CHAMPIONS OF FREEDOM

The Ludwig von Mises Lecture Series

CHAMPIONS OF FREEDOM
Volume 38

The New Deal

Gary Wolfram, Editor

Hillsdale College Press
Hillsdale, Michigan 49242

Hillsdale College Press

CHAMPIONS OF FREEDOM
The Ludwig von Mises Lecture Series—Volume 38
The New Deal

©2011 Hillsdale College Press, Hillsdale, Michigan 49242

First printing 2011

The views expressed in this volume are not necessarily the views of Hillsdale College.

Printed in the United States of America

Front cover: "Ring Around a Roosevelt Pockets Full of Dough"
          Clifford Kennedy Berryman, May 26, 1938
          © Corbis

Library of Congress Control Number: 2010940613

ISBN 978-0-916308-31-5

Contents

RECOMMENDED READINGS

From *Economic Freedom and Interventionism*
Ludwig von Mises

Contributors

Henry William Brands is the Dickson Allen Anderson Centennial Professor of History at the University of Texas at Austin, where he earned his doctorate in history. Dr. Brands has been an oral historian at the University of Texas Law School, and he has taught history at Vanderbilt University and Texas A&M University. A finalist for the Pulitzer Prize and the Lionel Gelber Prize in international affairs, he is a recipient of the Deolece Parmelee Award. He is a member of various honorary societies, including the Society of American Historians and the Philosophical Society of Texas. A regular guest on radio and television, he has written for the *New York Times*, *The Wall Street Journal*, *The Atlantic*, *The Journal of American History*, and *Political Science Quarterly*, among many others. He is author or editor of numerous books, including *Andrew Jackson*, *The Age of Gold*, *The First American*, and *Traitor to His Class: The Privileged Life and Radical Presidency of Franklin Delano Roosevelt*.

Alan Brinkley is the Allan Nevins Professor of History at Columbia University. Dr. Brinkley received his A.B. from Princeton and his Ph.D. from Harvard. He has taught previously at MIT, Harvard, the City University of New York Graduate School, and Oxford University. He is the recipient of numerous fellowships and awards, including the Great Teacher Award at Columbia. He is chairman of the board of trustees of the Century Foundation, a trustee of the National Humanities Center, a trustee of Oxford University Press, and a member of the American Academy of Arts and Sciences. His writing has appeared in numerous scholarly and popular journals, including the *New York Review of Books*, *The New Yorker*, the *New York Times Book Review*, and *The New Republic*. His books include *Voices of Protest: Huey Long, Father Coughlin, and the Great Depression*, which won the 1983 National Book Award; *The End of Reform: New Deal Liberalism in Recession and War*; *Liberalism and Its Discontents*; and *Franklin Delano Roosevelt*.

Burton Folsom, Jr., studied at Centre College before receiving his B.A. at Indiana University. Dr. Folsom holds a master's degree from the University of Nebraska and a Ph.D. from the University of Pittsburgh. He has taught at Murray State University, Northwood University, and currently holds the Charles Kline Chair in History and Management at Hillsdale College. He also worked for several years at the Mackinac Center for Public Policy and the Center for the American Idea. He is currently a guest scholar at the Heritage Foundation, senior historian at the Foundation for Economic Education, and writes a quarterly column for *The Freeman*. His articles have appeared in *The Wall Street Journal*, *Business History Review*, *Investor's Business Daily*, and the *Washington Times*, among others. He has made numerous radio and television appearances, including *The Glenn Beck Program*, *FOX & Friends*, and C-SPAN. He has published six books, including *Myth of the Robber Barons* and *New Deal or Raw Deal? How FDR's Economic Legacy Has Damaged America*.

Charles R. Kesler is the Dengler-Dykema Distinguished Professor of Government at Claremont McKenna College. Dr. Kesler received his Ph.D. in government from Harvard University. He is editor of the *Claremont Review of Books* and a senior fellow of the Claremont Institute. He has previously served as director of the Henry Salvatori Center at Claremont McKenna College, as Vice Chairman of the Advisory Committee to the official U.S. James Madison Commemoration Commission, and as a member of the Thomas Jefferson–Sally Hemings Scholars Commission. His articles on contemporary politics have appeared in *The Wall Street Journal*, *Policy Review*, *National Review*, *The Weekly Standard*, and other journals. His edition of *The Federalist*

Papers is the best-selling edition in the country. He is the editor of and a contributor to *Saving the Revolution: The Federalist Papers and the American Founding*, and he is co-editor, with the late William F. Buckley, Jr., of *Keeping the Tablets: Modern American Conservative Thought*.

Larry Schweikart is a professor of history at the University of Dayton. Dr. Schweikart received his B.A. and M.A. degrees from Arizona State University, and a Ph.D. in history from the University of California, Santa Barbara. He has previously taught at UC Santa Barbara and the University of Wisconsin. He has made numerous radio and television appearances, including FOX News, *The Glenn Beck Program*, *FOX & Friends*, Al Jazeera, and C-SPAN. He has written for various publications, including *The Freeman* and *Investor's Business Daily*. The author of many scholarly and popular articles and reviews on economics, business, and banking, his books include *The Entrepreneurial Adventure: A History of American Enterprise*; *America's Victories: Why the U.S. Wins Wars*; *48 Liberal Lies About American History*; *Seven Events that Made America America*; and *A Patriot's History of the United States: From Columbus's Great Discovery to the War on Terror* (co-authored with Michael Allen).

Amity Shlaes is a senior fellow in economic history at the Council on Foreign Relations. She is also a columnist for Bloomberg News. A graduate of Yale University, she pursued postgraduate studies at the Free University in Berlin. Ms. Shlaes has served as a member of the editorial board of *The Wall Street Journal* and as a columnist for the *Financial Times*. In 2009 she was winner of the Hayek Prize, a book prize from the Thomas Smith Foundation of the Manhattan Institute. In 2003 she was the J. P. Morgan Fellow in Finance and Economics at the American Academy in Berlin. In 2002 she was co-winner of the Frederic Bastiat Prize, an international award for free-market journalism. She is the author of two national bestsellers, *The Greedy Hand: A Profile of the Tax Code* and *The Forgotten Man: A New History of the Great Depression*. She is currently at work on a biography of Calvin Coolidge.

Bradley C. S. Watson is professor of political science at Saint Vincent College in Latrobe, Pennsylvania, where he holds the Philip M. McKenna Chair in American and Western Political Thought. He has held visiting faculty appointments at Princeton University and Claremont McKenna College. Dr. Watson serves as senior scholar at the Intercollegiate Studies Institute and on the boards of the National Association of Scholars and the Association for the Study of Free Institutions. He has received fellowships from numerous organizations, including the National Endowment for the Humanities, Earhart Foundation, the Heritage Foundation, the John M. Olin Foundation, the Foundation for the Defense of Democracies, and the John Templeton Foundation. He has appeared on many radio programs and on *The Glenn Beck Program* on the FOX News Channel. He has authored or edited numerous books, including *Living Constitution, Dying Faith: Progressivism and the New Science of Jurisprudence.*

Introduction

The 2010 Ludwig von Mises lecture series could not have been more timely. As the U.S. and world economies recover from the recent financial crisis, a resurgence in interest in the Great Depression and the New Deal has taken hold. There is good reason for this. While we are not likely to suffer the reduction in economic activity that occurred during the Depression, the media as well as some economists were, and some still are, predicting such. Indeed, the conservative author Richard Posner of the University of Chicago, who blogs with Nobel Laureate Gary Becker, has written a popular book titled *A Failure of Capitalism: The Crisis of '08 and the Descent into Depression* (Cambridge, MA: Harvard University Press, 2009).

Can we look to the Great Depression of 1929 for answers to our current crisis—why it occurred and what actions we need to take to move the economy back to its former growth path? Was the New Deal successful, such that it can serve as a model of what we should do, or was it unsuccessful in a way that can tell us what not to do? Is President Obama pursuing and likely to pursue further a political agenda that is reminiscent of that of Franklin Roosevelt, and what does this say about our political and economic freedom and the role of government in our social order? The papers in this volume of Champions of Freedom provide a basis for the answers to these important questions.

Both the Great Depression and the fiscal crisis of 2007–2009 have been characterized by the media and those who wish to expand the role of government as a failure of capitalism. However, Austrian business cycle theory, as developed by Ludwig von Mises, explains that bubbles and recessions, and depressions for that matter, are the result of governmental interference in markets, in particular the market for loanable funds. This leads to what Friedrich Hayek called malinvestment, the misdirection of resources into sectors of the economy for which there is no sustainable consumer demand. The housing bubble that collapsed in 2006 and the recession that followed is a prototype recession, with the Federal Reserve lowering the federal funds rates well below the market equilibrium and holding it there for a year. The malinvestment occurred in housing this time due to the government policy of expanding home ownership to those who couldn't actually afford it, through programs such as those of Fannie Mae, Freddie Mac, and the amendments to the Community Reinvestment Act. The end result, while not on the scale of the Great Depression, has been one of the most severe bouts of unemployment since that time. As with the Great Depression, the cause of our economic downturn lies with government action and not the capitalist system.

The lectures at the Mises program shed light on the philosophical underpinnings of the New Deal, the political realignments that it engendered, and the direct and indirect economic effects of the plethora of programs adopted by FDR. They addressed the personal attributes of FDR and the effect he and his programs have had on the role of the federal government. They will also allow us to sort out the policies of the Bush and Obama administrations in response to the recent recession and their effect on the U.S. economy and political landscape.

In "The Life and Times of FDR," H. W. Brands examines the psychological impact of the Roosevelt presidency, emphasizing FDR's skill as a communicator and his ability to influence public opinion. Roosevelt used the then-new medium of radio to enter the living rooms of the American public in a way not done before or since. Brands addresses the issue of why Roosevelt is such a polarizing figure today, arguing that much of it has to do with our view of the success or failure of the New Deal. He argues that FDR and the New Deal did not extend the Depression, and that those who do believe that are basing their opinion on faith, not evidence. Finally, Brands holds

Roosevelt up as one of two presidents, the other being Lincoln, who had the greatest effect on how Americans live today. Through the actions of the Roosevelt administration, Americans now expect their government to step in to address economic problems and we are no longer an isolationist nation.

In "The Intellectual Roots of the New Deal," Bradley Watson lays out the philosophical background that led to the pragmatic experimentalism of the Roosevelt administration. He contrasts the belief of Lincoln in the founding principles and natural rights with the speeches of Roosevelt that demonstrate FDR's belief in an organic state to be unencumbered by constitutional limitations. In a detailed discussion of Social Darwinism, Watson lays out the foundation for the Progressive movement that came to fruition in the Roosevelt presidency. He outlines how Social Darwinist thought led political thinkers to adopt the belief in an ever-adapting and growing state, one unbound by political truths and limitations and led by an elite class of thinkers. Watson then goes on to describe how Progressivism combined Social Darwinism with the philosophy of Pragmatism, as expounded by William James and, particularly, John Dewey. This led to the New Deal's ripening of the Progressive fruit in the substitution of political expertise for the invisible hand of the market place, and the growth of federal programs and the administrative state all in the name of change. This legacy of the New Deal is today a defining characteristic of the Obama presidency.

Alan Brinkley, in "Legacies of the New Deal," provides us with what he sees as the five legacies of the New Deal. These are a reformulation of the political landscape, with the Roosevelt policies establishing the Democratic Party as the party of Progressives, pulling blacks away from the Republican Party, and creating powerful labor unions as a major force within the Democratic Party. The physical landscape was changed by the public works construction—from roads and bridges to libraries and rural electrification. The modern welfare state emerges from the Social Security Act of 1935. The New Deal established the idea that capitalism is imbedded with fundamental flaws that government must correct. The final legacy is the establishment of presidential leadership as embodied by a pragmatic flexibility and willingness to act aggressively in the face of national crisis, whether that action is thought out or not.

Burt Folsom, in "Keynesianism and the Economic Principles of the New Deal," provides descriptions of the failures of the New Deal programs, which would be humorous if not so tragic. In one example he describes the workings of the Agricultural Adjustment Act, which paid farmers not to farm. Because some farmers would cheat—take the money and plant crops anyway—we hired inspectors to check on them. Because some inspectors would take bribes and look the other way, the government hired inspectors to check on the inspectors. We reduced the acreage cultivated with the result that two years later we have a crop shortage and are forced to import millions of bushels of corn, wheat, and cotton. Somehow this program was supposed to get us out of the Depression. Folsom details other programs with wit and insight, and demonstrates that the New Deal was an abject failure. The high taxes stifled innovation. Perhaps the most interesting point Folsom makes is how Roosevelt used these programs to spread federal largess to politically important districts, in effect bribing voters with tax dollars. He closes with an argument that implementing tax cuts rather than increasing federal spending is the way to create economic growth and advance freedom.

Amity Shlaes, in "The Rules of the Game and Economic Recovery," draws attention to the myths that surround the Great Depression, using the concept of the board game *Monopoly* to make her point. Her research has shown that the policies of the Roosevelt administration made things worse rather than better. The destruction of property rights and the lack of clarity in the rules of the game caused an "investment strike." Her analysis is consistent with that of Robert Higgs who wrote of the "regime uncertainty" of the Roosevelt administration leading to a collapse of private investment. The solution to the current crisis, Ms. Shlaes suggests, is to recognize that property rights and rule of law are fundamental to economic growth and recovery—a lesson that can be learned from a proper study of the New Deal.

Larry Schweikart, in "The Economic and Political Legacy of the New Deal," discusses both the economic and political legacy of the New Deal. Referring to his earlier work, he demonstrates how the numerous New Deal programs not only failed to accomplish their short-term goals, but caused long-term damage to the economy. Schweikart expresses exasperation with the treatment that historians have given Roosevelt, arguing that they have perpetuated a story of success that is unfounded and in contradiction to what most economists think. He argues, in opposition to Brinkley, that getting off the gold standard and establishing the FDIC were destabilizing factors. The Roosevelt "Brains Trust" was Keynesian in its outlook, which led to all the "make work" programs of the New Deal. This led to one of the chief legacies of the New Deal, the complete makeover of the concept of the dignity and value of work. Rather than seeing work as having value when it produces goods and services for others, we began to see the act of work as a way to create value in the Marxian sense. Another legacy was the idea the government should set prices and output. Historians fail to connect the artificial increases in wages due to various FDR programs with the stubbornly high unemployment rate of the entire New Deal period. Finally Schweikart reiterates Burt Folsom's point that every New Deal program had a political as well as an economic purpose, which was to establish the Democratic Party as the majority party far into the future.

Charles Kesler, in "The New New Deal," provides an excellent comparison of FDR and Barack Obama, their programs and philosophy. Kesler notes that the New Deal, while a novel expansion of the role of the federal government, was popular at the time. This is in contrast with President Obama's New New Deal, which has been unpopular not just with Republicans, but also with independents and Democrats. FDR brought about the concept of rights to be provided by government rather than unalienable rights protected by government. Obama's programs enshrine some of these rights into law, fulfilling some of the old promises of the New Deal. However, while FDR can be thought of as a Progressive, Kesler shows how Obama adds a postmodernist philosophy to the liberalism of the New Deal. This results in a president who rejects absolute truths and, as Kesler puts it, is uncomfortable with America's exceptionalism—"and thus with America itself."

Government often expands during an economic crisis as politicians blame the unemployment that is the inevitable result of the central bank's expansion of credit on "corporate greed." Like Roosevelt before him, President Obama has blamed our current economic crisis on Wall Street and has used the power of the federal government to invade property rights and create uncertainty in what are the rules of the game. This in turn has led, as in the Great Depression, to a reduction in private investment, high and persistent unemployment, and a drag on the economy. The readers of this volume will be better-armed to understand this pattern of what Robert Higgs has termed "Crisis and Leviathan" and to defend our system of market capitalism and limited government against the inroads of those who would restrain our liberty.

GARY WOLFRAM
William Simon Professor of
Economics and Public Policy
Hillsdale College

H. W. BRANDS

The Life and Times of FDR

I am going to try to recreate for you the essential moment at the beginning of Franklin Roosevelt's administration—the one moment that captured the possibilities of the New Deal, that captured the imagination of the American people, and that captured for historians the secret of Roosevelt's political success. Franklin Delano Roosevelt became president of the United States in March of 1933. For the previous three months the American banking system had been in free fall. As people began to lose confidence in the banking system, one by one—and then dozen by dozen, and score by score, and hundreds by hundreds—banks began to close, taking the depositors' money with them. Honest, hardworking citizens by the millions were in despair as they realized their life savings were gone.

When a bank folded in those days, there was no recourse. Say you were 65 years old in 1933 and about to retire. Over your entire working life, some forty years, you had diligently put money into a bank account, where it was supposed to be safe and available when you needed. You had not played the stock market, like so many reckless people had in the 1920s. Their money was already gone, wiped out in the stock crash of 1929. You had done all the right things. You had planned and saved for your future. But now your money was gone, too.

The first thing that Roosevelt did upon becoming president was to declare a banking holiday—a wonderful euphemism. This "holiday" was to allow the banking system and the bankers and the depositors time to catch their breath. He didn't actually seize the banks, he didn't take them over, he simply said there will be no more banking until I say there will be banking. It was a drastic step, but not without precedent (and it is interesting that nothing like this was proposed during the financial crisis of 2008). Earlier in 1933, the governor of Michigan had closed that state's banks, as had governors of 18 other states. By closing the nation's banks, Roosevelet simply nationalized an action that had been going on for awhile.

The next thing he did was summon a special session of Congress. Nowadays Congress is nearly always in session, but in the nineteenth and early twentieth centuries, members of Congress spent far more time at home in their districts and states than they spent in Washington. In fact, being a member of Congress used to be a distinctly part-time occupation. And a lot of people thought the country was better governed when Congress was in Washington less frequently than it is now. In 1933 Congress met to swear in new members and to inaugurate the new president (which occurred on March 4). Then they went home, planning not to return until December.

For a president, there are advantages and disadvantages to this approach. The disadvantage is that Congress isn't around to pass laws as necessary. The advantage is that Congress isn't around to get in your way. Roosevelt needed Congress in session because he needed them to pass emergency banking legislation.

When Roosevelt asked Congress to pass what became the Emergency Banking Act of 1933, not only had Congress members not read the bill, they couldn't read it, since the actual copies of the bill were still being printed. However, the country was in such despair that Americans, and certainly Congress, which had large Democratic majorities in both houses, were willing to give Roosevelt pretty much whatever he wanted.

Contrast this to the summer of 2009 when the health reform bill was being debated. Congress members went back to their constituencies and were greeted by vocal opponents of the reform who made much of the fact that the bill was long and complicated. These opponents would confront their member of Congress at rallies and chant: "Read the bill, read the bill." What these protestors were questioning was how Congress could vote on a bill the members of Congress had not read.

The most quoted line from Franklin Roosevelt's first inaugural address is "We have nothing to fear but fear itself." However, it is important to know that the line that caught people's attention back then captured a strikingly different mood. FDR said "We have nothing to fear but fear itself" at the beginning of his address, basically telling everyone to calm down, that everything was going to be okay. But at the end of his speech, he likened the economic crisis to a state of war. He said that the powers he would require to deal with it were very much like the powers of a commander-in-chief during wartime. FDR did, in fact, ask for that kind of authority—and Congress was willing to hand it to him.

The Emergency Banking Act specified how the government was to shore up the financial system. It explained how the banks would be reopened and it offered a timetable for their reopening. This occurred on the Friday after Roosevelt's inauguration (which had taken place the previous Saturday). The banks were to start reopening on Monday, but the critical moment came not with the vote on Friday nor with the scheduled bank reopenings on Monday. The critical moment came on Sunday night, the night that Roosevelt commandeered the airwaves and gave a radio address. For a president to address a national audience was rare in those days. Television broadcasts, of course, did not yet exist, and no preceding president had made use of radio, the principle medium of the day, to the extent and with the effectiveness that Roosevelt would. Roosevelt had decided that he wasn't going to give an address or a lecture—it was going to be a chat, the first of FDR's Fireside Chats. It was scheduled for 10 p.m. eastern standard time on a cold Sunday night in the depths of the Depression. Many people had already gone to bed (mostly in order to conserve fuel), but they could still listen to the radio.

A striking thing about radio is its intimacy. Reading a book requires participation: You have to create the characters in your head. The same is true when listening to the radio. Most of the 70 million people who heard Roosevelt that night had never seen him other than in a photograph, which doesn't really convey a full impression of the personality. And unlike the usual political rhetoric, a speaker doesn't have to "orate" on the radio, doesn't have to project. In fact, on radio, a person can speak very softly—and it will sound, to the listener, as if that the person is speaking just to you.

I study history in part because I like stories about the past, but I have long had a side interest in mathematics and science. One thing that has frustrated me about history is that you don't get to conduct experiments. But as I was researching my book on FDR, I realized I could: I could recreate the conditions of the first Fireside Chat. Through the miracle of the Internet, you can hear Franklin Roosevelt speak. So I waited until a cold night in winter. I turned out the lights and went to bed—but with my laptop, not a radio, at my bedside. Franklin Roosevelt spoke for just fourteen and a half minutes in that first chat, but in that brief time he explained the nature of the banking industry. He explained how it was supposed to work. He explained what had gone wrong. He explained what his administration had done and what Congress had done. He outlined the basics of the Emergency Banking Act. He explained that there was a timetable for reopening the banks. Some banks would reopen the next morning at ten o'clock; another round of banks would open on Tuesday; and the rest of the banks would open on Wednesday.

After he explained everything, he did something that was key to Roosevelt's success. He explained to the American people that everything that had been done in Washington and everything that had been done in on Wall Street would be for nothing without the support, without the cooperation, without the faith and confidence of the American people. This is particularly true of banking, as Roosevelt knew. Basically he was telling Americans that without their support we can do nothing, with their support there is nothing we cannot do.

Once as I described this first Fireside Chat in a lecture, I said that when people listened to Roosevelt—when I listened to Roosevelt in my experiment—it was very easy to imagine that the voice you were hearing was not the voice of the president of the United States, not the voice of someone thousands of miles away, but the voice of your father, or your grandfather, or your favorite uncle telling you that that everything is going to be okay. Many people had that reaction. One woman raised her hand and said: "You know, the voice of Roosevelt wasn't like the voice of my father. It wasn't like the voice of my grandfather. It was the voice of God."

There is a common misconception that FDR's fireside chats were the same as the weekly presidential radio addresses that have been a standard feature of American political life since Richard Nixon was in the White House—the ones no one listens to. No one listens partly because they are weekly, and largely because presidents now have many other, more effective ways to get the word out. Franklin Roosevelt gave a total of forty fireside chats during his twelve years as president. Each one was considered a really big deal, and people paid attention to them. These chats made it seem that FDR himself had come into their homes, that he had become like a member of the family. Through them he was able to forge a special connection with the American people.

Roosevelt's first fireside chat ended at 10:15 that Sunday night; the banks were scheduled to open twelve hours later. Every day for the previous three months, lines had formed outside the banks, which lead the bank presidents, the bank employees, and all the neighbors to think, "Oh my God, this is it: The bank is going to close." That was because those lines were filled with depositors who were trying to get their money out. The Monday morning after FDR's first fireside chat, lines formed again. And, again, bank presidents said, "Oh, lordy, the end is nigh." But when the banks opened their doors, the strangest thing happened. Instead of withdrawing money, people came to make deposits, returning what they had previously withdrawn and put under their mattresses. It was a nationwide vote of confidence in Franklin Roosevelt. The secret of Roosevelt's success was his ability to make Americans believe that for the first time in their memory government was working on their behalf.

Remember that when Roosevelt became president, the general belief was that a person's life was essentially of his or her own doing. There was a fundamental divide between the operations of the private economy and the operations of the government. There was the private sector and there was government, and while I wouldn't say ne'er the twain should meet, they didn't meet often and only under very unusual circumstances. Also, there was a notion back then that the business cycle was like the weather. You could complain about it, but you couldn't do anything about it. There were boom times when everybody was happy

and got rich, and there were bad times when people suffered depriva-
tions. If you found yourself in the middle of a bad time, your job was to
tighten your belt and hope and pray that the good times would return.
The goods times had always returned in the past, but in the 1930s, their
comeback was taking a long time.

Many people believe that Roosevelt set the United States on a
path that has led us away from American traditions, away from the
values and practices that made America great. Some believe that if we
could undo the New Deal, if somehow we could get back on the track
we were on in the 1920s and early 1930s, the country would be much
better off. Some think that Roosevelt and the New Deal did not end
the Great Depression, but instead aggravated it and extended it. There
is some evidence supporting this position, which is, I would say, a core
principle of conservative belief in this country.

Franklin Roosevelt remains a polarizing figure. Theodore Roosevelt was just as controversial in his day as FDR was in his but I can't
start a fight, I can't start even a debate, about Teddy Roosevelt's positions on matters. Everyone loves him. Republicans love him despite
the fact that most Republicans of his time hated him; Democrats love
him despite the fact the he was a Republican. So why is it that a discussion of Franklin Roosevelt can still turn into a brawl? I would say this
is true in large part because we may be on the verge of a New Deal
2.0. For a while it looked as though we might be on the verge of Great
Depression 2.0.

The belief that Franklin Roosevelt and the New Deal extended
the Great Depression is wrong. I can't prove definitively that it is wrong
because, for those who know the rules of logic, the proposition that the
New Deal extended the Great Depression begins with a counterfactual.
It begins by negating the premise. You can prove anything you want if
you negate the premise, but the results are neither sound nor convincing.
And, I should also add, in history arguments are never proved.

Looking at the history of the business cycle from the beginning
of the twentieth century until today, and examining its course and
the timing between the precipitant of the current crisis and the crash
of 1929—and the bottom of the downturn that follows, whether a
recession or depression—that time frame is typically about $2\frac{1}{2}$ years.
After that things begin to get better. Thus one could conclude from

this that Roosevelt became president about 2½ years after the stock market crashed—just when things should have been getting better on their own—and he institutes the New Deal. This scares investors who can't figure out what to do, so they stay on the sidelines and the market doesn't turn upward again.

Herbert Hoover stepped off the American political stage after his defeat by Roosevelt in 1932, but he lived into the 1960s. He went to his grave convinced that he had solved the riddle of the Great Depression, and that the economy had been improving. If the American people had only had the good sense to reelect him, all would have been well. Even though there had been a slight uptick in the stock market and some other indices in the summer and early fall of 1932, FDR won the election, scaring the investors.

There is a fundamental problem with this argument about the timing of the Depression and the timing of the business cycle. The problem is that most of the data points in this model come from the period *after* the New Deal. Most business recessions occurred between the 1930s to the present. So to say that because the average length of these post-Great Depression recessions was 2½ years, the length of the Great Depression should have been 2½ years is to ignore everything that was done by the New Deal that had served to ameliorate, or perhaps to prevent, future depressions.

In FDR's day, the evidence ran in the opposite direction. FDR was born in 1882, near the beginning of the accelerating phase of the American industrial revolution. He was just a kid when the depression of the 1890s came along. There had been a panic in 1873, which led to a depression that lasted about three years. In 1893 there was another financial panic that led to a four-year depression. There was a panic in 1907 that didn't lead to a depression. Then, in 1929, there was the Great Depression, which lasted until Roosevelt became president in 1933. The pattern seemed to be that industrial capitalism kept lurching from boom to bust and the busts kept getting deeper and longer. By 1933, 25 percent of the workforce was unemployed.

New Deal legislation did much to ensure there would be no future depressions. I will discuss just a few of its actions.

The basic difference between the banking crisis of 1932–1933 and the banking crisis of 2008 is that in 2008 not a single bank depositor lost a nickel. It was a crisis for banks and bank shareholders, but shareholders are aware that investing in stock exposes their money to risk. That it was not a crisis for depositors—who, unlike investors, seek security for their savings—was because of the Federal Deposit Insurance Corporation, which was created in FDR's first 100 days. The FDIC is why you can sleep soundly each night, knowing that your savings are safe. The reason there has been no repetition of the stock market crash of 1929—and why the closest thing to it occurred in 2007–2008—is because of another law passed in 1933, the Glass-Stegell Act. It prevented the corner bank from taking your deposits and playing the stock market—with its inherent, and acknowledged, risks—with them. For the 66 years it was on the books, this act prevented a recurrence of the financial meltdown of the early 1930s. In 1999 Glass-Stegell was repealed, and banks and financial institution, now more broadly defined, began doing exactly what banks had been doing in the 1920s. As the inevitable financial failures became evident, the Fed and the Treasury had to declare certain banks "too big to fail." Had those banks been allowed to fail, they would have brought down the rest of the economy.

Many countries got themselves out of the Depression by means of—what term shall I use?—economic stimulus packages. Germany instituted the first economic stimulus package in the 1930s, focusing on rearmament. Hitler built up the German Army, Navy and Air Force, and this military spending pulled Germany out of the Depression. Britain came out of the Depression next, in 1937. The British government also spent heavily on rearmament, in response to Germany. What pulled the United States out of the Depression? An economic stimulus package. It was government spending on war materiels—on the production of tanks and airplanes and ships and the rest.

Franklin Roosevelt was one of two great presidents in American history, the other being Abraham Lincoln. Both were great in the very literal sense of having had the greatest effect on the way Americans subsequently lived. I grew up in Oregon and I thought, naively, that there was a consensus that Abraham Lincoln and his policies had been good for the country. Then I moved to Texas and discovered that there was no consensus on this. Plenty of people in Texas and throughout the south think that Abraham Lincoln did not do the right things. The same is true of Franklin Roosevelt.

Franklin Roosevelt changed Americans' expectations of their government at home and he changed Americans' expectations of their
country's role in the world. When Roosevelt became president, Americans didn't expect much from their government, especially regarding
the actions and the behavior of the economy. By the time Roosevelt
left office, Americans expected that when the economy was performing
poorly, the government would step in and do something about it.

I contend that Americans have never seriously reconsidered this
opinion. If anything, the consensus behind this Rooseveltian worldview
is stronger now than it was when Roosevelt died in 1945. Proof positive of this is that in 2008, when the financial sector was on the verge
of collapse, a Republican president and his Republican administration
and most Republicans in Congress said that the government had to step
in and prevent the meltdown. Remember that it was George W. Bush
and his administration that proposed buying up toxic assets, that took
the steps that nearly everyone believed were necessary to shore up the
financial sector. This was not something Herbert Hoover would have
done. This was not something that presidents before Roosevelt would
have done. But after Franklin Roosevelt, presidents, liberal and conservative alike, have taken the view that the economy is the responsibility of
the government. For better or worse, this is the world that we live in.

The America Roosevelt inherited in 1933 was reflexively, almost
irretrievably, isolationist. Americans believed that what happened in
East Africa, what happened in Eastern Europe, what happened in East
Asia could safely be ignored by the American people. The world might
go to hell in a handbasket, but Americans could stay on the sidelines.
It took Roosevelt nine years to persuade Americans that this was very
shortsighted. And it was not until the Japanese attacked Pearl Harbor
at the end of 1941 did Americans as a group finally come to realize
that the United States does need to be aware of what is going on in the
world, that threats to democracy anywhere are potentially threats to
American democracy at home. Again, I point to recent evidence that
Americans have never seriously reconsidered this aspect of the Rooseveltian worldview. In 1925, to pick a date before Roosevelt became
president, it would have boggled the mind of nearly any American
to think that American troops would ever be fighting wars in Iraq or
Afghanistan. But there they are, and, again, remember they were sent

not by a Democratic or liberal administration: They were sent by the most conservative Republican administration we have had in a long time. This simply underscores how Roosevelt's presidency changed the world.

BRADLEY C. S. WATSON

The Intellectual Roots of the New Deal

Examining the intellectual roots of the New Deal is a substantial task, to put it mildly. It requires channeling a large river with many tributaries. For purposes of contrast and clarity, it is useful to begin this channeling by casting our minds back to an age that antecedes the New Deal, and to those ideas that can rightly be considered its intellectual roots.

In 1863, Abraham Lincoln reminded his listeners that America "was conceived in liberty, and dedicated to the proposition that all men are created equal." Earlier, Lincoln had proclaimed that all living Americans are the "legal inheritors" of the "fundamental blessings" bequeathed by the founders—whose principles, institutions, and very names we have a duty to preserve. The principles must be preserved because they are true, because they are in conformity with the cause of civil liberty, of natural rights. Thus they must shine on, according to Lincoln, in "naked deathless splendor." The political rhetoric and actions of Lincoln remain among the greatest statements that there are such things as natural rights that do not change with time, and that the American Constitution is dedicated to preserving them. Thus the task of great political actors, while responding to urgent necessities, is to look

11

backward as much as—perhaps more than—forward. For Lincoln, the state is more formal than organic; history is not destined to unfold in a democratic direction; and democracy itself, because of its indissoluble link with the passions rather than reason, is always combustible.

Moral and political regress are as likely as progress. Furthermore, there are certain fixed principles beyond which progress is impossible. Sharing with Plato and Aristotle the belief that negative regime change is an ever-present possibility, Lincoln was profoundly wary of the very notion of progress; evolution and growth were not part of his political vocabulary. The job of government, mainly and simply, is to protect the prepolitical rights given us by the laws of nature and nature's God.

In Lincoln we can see the culmination of the old understanding of the American constitutional order and the political principles it enshrined. Lincoln's articulation of the nature and purposes of the American regime was perhaps the high water mark of the old constitutionalism—that is to say, the preprogressive constitutionalism.

The new, progressive constitutionalism that would sweep the intellectual classes almost immediately after the Age of Lincoln led, in turn, to the constitutionalism of the New Deal. Indeed, by 1932 things had changed almost unrecognizably.

In that year, Franklin Delano Roosevelt, in his Commonwealth Club address, which he delivered on the campaign trail, called on Americans to engage in a "a re-appraisal of values." He told Americans that the "earlier concepts" of the American constitutional order had to be adapted—*ever* adapted—to suit the conditions of the day. In the course of doing that, he relied on a striking reconfiguration of the Founders' constitutionalism. He told his audience that "[t]he Declaration of Independence discusses the problem of Government in terms of a contract…. Under such a contract rulers were accorded power, and the people consented to that power on consideration that they be accorded certain rights. The task of statesmanship has always been the redefinition of these rights in terms of a changing and growing social order."

In this formulation, rights themselves are decidedly political rather than prepolitical: They are gifts of government, not God, and therefore eminently negotiable, according to the exigencies of the age—of the changing and growing social order. Roosevelt also told Americans that their "task now is not discovery…or…producing more goods. It is the soberer, less dramatic business of administering resources and plants already in hand…of adjusting production to consumption, of distributing wealth and products more equitably." He announced that "The day of enlightened administration has come," in aid of "a more permanently safe order of things."

In words that sound remarkably contemporary, FDR went on to proclaim, "Every man has a right to life; and this means that he has also a right to make a comfortable living…. Every man has a right to his own property; which means a right to be assured, to the fullest extent attainable, in the safety of his savings…. If, in accord with this principle, we must restrict the operations of the speculator, the manipulator, even the financier, I believe we must accept the restriction as needful, not to hamper individualism but to protect it…. [T]he responsible heads of finance and industry, instead of acting each for himself, must work together to achieve the common end. They must, where necessary, sacrifice this or that private advantage; and in reciprocal self-denial must seek a general advantage. It is here that formal government—political government, if you choose—comes in."

A few years later, during his first term as president, Roosevelt offered these equally contemporary reflections in his 1935 address to the Young Democrats Clubs of America: This "modern economic world of ours is governed by rules and regulations vastly more complex than those laid down in the days of Adam Smith or John Stuart Mill…. Our concepts of the regulation of money and credit and industrial competition, of the relation of employer and employee created for the old civilization, are being modified to save our economic structure from confusion, destruction and paralysis…. Government cooperation to help make the system of free enterprise work, to provide that minimum security without which the competitive system cannot function, to restrain the kind of individual action which in the past has been harmful to the community—that kind of governmental cooperation is entirely consistent with the best tradition of America."

Nowadays, of course, when our current president utters such lines, they indeed ring true—or truer—than they did in FDR's time. Such federal government "cooperation" to restrain individual action does indeed seem consistent with a tradition that has existed in America *since* the New Deal.

However, it is not clear that such a tradition existed *prior* to the New Deal—hence FDR's much greater boldness, and much greater inventiveness, in speaking with a straight face about such a tradition, compared to Barack Obama's far more platitudinous invocations of that tradition.

In his famous Four Freedoms speech, FDR assured us that we were moving rapidly toward a future that promised to look like the one in Tolstoy's legend of the green stick—where universal happiness and ease would be realized. The millenarian hopes of mankind could be attained with the revelation of…something, in History. Universal freedom *of* speech and worship, and *from* want and fear are, in FDR's words, "no vision of a distant millennium. It is a definite basis for a kind of world attainable in our own time and generation." As our current president is wont to say, "This is our moment. This is our time."

But just how did we move so far so fast, how did we get from one to the other—from Abraham Lincoln to FDR—in twenty years fewer than four score and seven?

American political thought subsequent to Lincoln for the most part has amounted to an attack on Lincoln's conception of American constitutionalism and the philosophical proposition on which it rests. This transformation in political thought, commencing after Reconstruction and running through the progressive era of the early twentieth century, undergirds many forms of political action in America to this day.

In the America of the late nineteenth century, the old understanding of the nature and permanent limits of politics was dead or dying. We can summarize this transformation as a move away from the earlier constitutionalism of fixed principles, cognizable words, modest executive and judicial branches, and the limits imposed by federalism, to an organic or progressive constitutionalism in which the very notion of fixity or constitutional principle is something that must be overcome.

The transformation rests on the coalescing of two important strains of American political thought—social Darwinism and pragmatism—

into a powerful intellectual force that decisively informed institutional and political attitudes and behaviors starting in the early twentieth century. The doctrines merged by the early twentieth century into the political and intellectual movement known as progressivism, which is really nothing more than the politicization of these twin doctrines.

In this view, intelligent guidance and endless socio-political reform are always possible because no problem is understood to be an inherent facet of human nature. This understanding alone is sufficient to distinguish social Darwinism or pragmatism from the political science of *The Federalist*—and the Founders' Constitution.

Many of the great progressive thinkers, such as Woodrow Wilson, were rather explicitly contemptuous, we might say, of the American constitutional order, which they understood as embodying Newtonian, mechanical ideas and institutions that stand in the way of necessary and vital organic growth. At various times in his life, Wilson himself advocated constitutional revolution, whether in the form of a modified parliamentary system, or in a more diluted form of strong executive leadership of Congress. All this in aid of providing centralized command and control mechanisms that, under the anachronistic eighteenth-century system of limited and diffuse powers—the system of the Founders—could not coalesce and become a necessary vanguard for the direction of an ever-evolving Constitution that must change with history.

Wilson's reform ideas were at best partially successful. Presidents, and congresses, have proved not quite powerful enough and—in the view of progressives—too beholden to populist sentiments that themselves reflect outmoded understandings of politics.

As the twentieth century wore on, the judiciary was tasked to take up the mantle of the most cutting-edge progressive reform. The shifting institutional allegiances of enlightened thinkers—away from faith in the ability of the executive and legislative branches to be in the vanguard of change and experimentation, and toward faith in judiciary to do the same job, only better—is a residue of the New Deal era.

This progressive-historicist view of the Constitution that, I claim, is at the heart of the New Deal is not simply that we have, of necessity, an interpretable Constitution, but one that must be interpreted in light of a particular understanding of the historically situated, contingent nature of the state, the individual, society, and constitutionalism itself. This understanding is in a considerable amount of tension with the earlier American constitutionalism of limited and dispersed powers serving the "laws of nature and nature's God." As Herman Belz has noted,

> The conception of the constitution as a formal legal instrument or code giving existence to government and prescribing and limiting the exercise of its powers, rather than as the basic structure of the polity, not consciously constructed but growing organically through history, was one of the distinctive achievements of the American Revolution, and oriented constitutional description and analysis in the early republic toward a legalistic approach.[1]

The modern historicist as opposed to legalistic approach has been embraced by elected officials, policymakers, and judicial appointees of different parties—Democrat and Republican, "liberal" and "conservative"—since the New Deal. It is now the unnoticed bedrock and background of American political consciousness. But it grew out of a particular time, place, and convergence of intellectual currents.

Let us consider in more detail the social Darwinist moment. As Richard Hofstadter has observed, "In some respects the United States during the last three decades of the nineteenth and at the beginning of the twentieth century was *the* social Darwinian country."[2]

According to the social Darwinists and those who would follow in their footsteps, a new social science was indebted to Darwin, whose organic, genetic, and experimental logic could be brought to bear on an array of human problems heretofore considered insoluble, or at least perennial. Darwin came to be understood as a political philosopher and political scientist rejecting old modes and orders.

No one more clearly explicates the nature of this new science than John Dewey in a great essay titled "The Influence of Darwinism on Philosophy."[3] By the time he wrote it in 1909, he was effectively summarizing the intellectual tenor of his times. He was giving an account of the origins of an already regnant pattern of American social and political thought.[4]

As Dewey avers, the publication of the *Origin of Species*—the first edition came out in 1859, and over the next dozen or so years five more editions were released—marked a revolution not only in the natural sciences, but in the human sciences as well, which could continue in their old form only under the pressures of habit and prejudice. In Dewey's words, "The influence of Darwin upon philosophy [and he might as well have said on politics and jurisprudence] resides in his having conquered the phenomena of life for the principle of transition, and thereby freed the new logic for application to mind and morals and life."

Darwin, more than anyone else, allows us to move from old questions that have lost their vital appeal to our perceived interests and needs. We do not solve old questions, according to Dewey, "[W]e get over them. Old questions are solved by disappearing, evaporating, while new questions corresponding to the changed attitude of endeavor and preference take their place. Doubtless the greatest dissolvent in contemporary thought of old questions, the greatest precipitant of new methods, new intentions, new problems, is the one effected by the scientific revolution that found its climax in the 'Origin of Species.'"

Dewey's Darwin lays hands "upon the sacred ark of permanency" that had governed our understanding of human beings. Darwin challenges the most sacred cow in the Western tradition, one that had been handed down from the Greeks: the belief in the "superiority of the fixed and final," including "the forms that had been regarded as types of fixity and perfection." The Greeks dilated on the characteristic traits of creatures, attaching the word species to them. As they manifested themselves in a completed form, or final cause, these species were seen to exhibit uniform structure and function, and to do so repeatedly, to the point where they were viewed as unchanging in their essential being. All changes were therefore held "within the metes and bounds of fixed truth."[5] Nature as a whole came to be viewed as "a progressive realization of purpose." The Greeks then propounded ethical systems based on purposiveness.

Henceforth, according to Dewey, "genetic" and "experimental" processes and methods can guide our inquiries into the human things.

In fact, on Darwinian terms, change is of the essence of the good, which is identified with organic adaptation, survival, and growth. With maximally experimental social arrangements, change in useless directions can quickly be converted into change in useful directions. The goal of philosophy is no longer to search after absolute origins or ends, but the processes that generate them.[6] What *materially* is becomes more important than what ought to be because only the former can be an object of the new empirical science.

In the absence of fixity, morals, politics, and religion are subject to radical renegotiation and transformation. Essences are no longer the highest object of inquiry, or indeed any object of inquiry. Rather, science concentrates on particular changes and their relationship to particular salutary purposes, which depend on "intelligent administration of existent conditions."[7]

Philosophy is reduced from the "wholesale" to the retail level.[8] Through the emphasis on administration of concrete conditions, Dewey claims responsibility is introduced to philosophy. Instead of concentrating on metaphysics, or even politics in the full Aristotelian sense, we are in effect freed to concentrate on policy—or, in Dewey's language, "the things that specifically concern us."

Darwin broke down the last barriers between scientific method and reconstruction in philosophy and the human sciences generally because of his overcoming of the view that human nature is different from the physical sciences and therefore requires a different approach. This is contrary to Aristotle's understanding that different methods of inquiry are required for different kinds of beings—there is no one scientific or philosophic mode of inquiry that applies across the board, though philosophy and science are seen as synonymous. Philosophy and science—the human striving after wisdom or knowledge—seeks an understanding of the highest things through an examination of all things, according to methods appropriate to each.

One way to understand Dewey's enterprise is to view it as an attempt to reintegrate science and philosophy, which had been torn asunder by modernity. While Dewey seeks their reintegration, he does so on uniquely modern terms—philosophy is reduced to empirical, naturalistic science—the processes, without the ends, or essences, or highest things.[9] We can therefore reduce human sciences, including politics, to relatively simple principles, contrary to the Aristotelian view, which held that politics is much harder than physics precisely because one must take into account unpredictable behavior, and choice-worthy, purposive behavior toward complex ends—rather than more predictable motions and processes toward simple ends. The human sciences, which at the highest level involve statesmanship, are, for Aristotle, more complex than the physical, and rely on great practical, experiential wisdom.[10] By contrast, for Dewey and his generation, Darwinism seemed to break down the barriers between the human and the nonhuman.

It should be noted that Dewey's elucidation of the utility of Darwinism to social science and the new philosophy of man abstracts from the thought of a number of the major social Darwinist thinkers, including William Graham Sumner, Lester Frank Ward, and W. E. B. DuBois. Together with Dewey, these men provided many of the intellectual categories of their age. And these categories continue to exert a powerful control over political and jurisprudential discourse to the present day. Collectively, they point to a view of society as an organism that, constantly in the throes of change, must grow or die. For the social Darwinists, to look backward—whether to founding principles or any other fixed standard of political right—inevitably reflects a death wish. While to some degree borrowing Hegelian historical categories, American social Darwinism shares no single rational end point with Hegelianism. Change in itself becomes the end in many instances, and is always preferable to its opposite.

Let me summarize these observations about the nature and influence of social Darwinism.

On the foundation laid by the social Darwinists and those in allied philosophical movements, in the twentieth century, many of the most influential American political thinkers and actors came to share six core, overlapping understandings of the nature of politics and constitutional government.

First, there are no fixed or eternal principles that govern, or ought to govern, the politics of a decent regime. Old political categories are just that, and Lincoln's understanding of the Founders' Constitution, to the extent it is worthy of any consideration, is a quaint anachronism.

Second, the state and its component parts are organic, each involved in a struggle for never-ending growth. Contrary to the Platonic ideal of *stasis*, and contrary too to the Aristotelian notion of natural movement toward particular ends, the new organic view of politics suggests movement itself is the key to survival and what can perhaps loosely be termed the political "good."

Third, democratic openness and experimentalism, in the economic but especially in the expressive realms, are necessary to ensure vigorous growth—they are the fertilizer of the organic state. Such experimentalism implies a particular sort of consequentialism or utilitarianism when judging institutions and laws.

Fourth, the state and its component parts exist only in History, understood as an inexorable process, rather than a mere record of events.

Fifth, some individuals stand outside this process and must, like captains of a great ship, periodically adjust the position of this ship in the river of History—to ensure that it continues to move forward, rather than run aground and stagnate. Politics demands an elite class, possessed of intelligence as a method, or reason directed to instrumental matters rather than fixed truth. This elite class springs into action to clear blockages in the path of historical progress, whether in the form of anachronistic institutions, laws, or ideas. These blockages will form in the path of the ship of state when openness or experimentalism proves inadequate. The brain-trusters and jurists become the philosopher kings of the new age.

Sixth, and a direct corollary to the strong historicism just mentioned, is that moral–political truth or rightness of action is always relative to one's moment in History, or the exact place of the ship in the river of time.

Despite its defining of so many of the terms of intellectual discourse in late nineteenth-century America, social Darwinism would not become known as the quintessential American philosophy. This honor belongs to pragmatism. However, the links between pragmatism and social Darwinism are wide and deep, and it is impossible to understand the "American philosophy" of pragmatism without understanding its relationship to social Darwinism. It is also impossible to dismiss social Darwinism's enduring influence on American political thought. The pragmatic tradition in fact worked "with the basic Darwinian concepts—organism, environment, adaptation," and spoke "the language of naturalism,"[11] as mentioned earlier.

William James's reflections on "What Pragmatism Means"[12] elucidate the links between these two schools of thought. Even though James rejected the Hegelian/Darwinian historical categories that were never far from the thinking of his fellow pragmatist and younger contemporary John Dewey, the two shared a thoroughgoing skepticism of the tradition of absolutes, a faith in progress, and an emphasis on the process, rather than essence, of human life and activity. With Darwinism, pragmatism rejects what James calls the "rationalist temper" that is ossifying rather than instrumental, and accepts the displacement of design from scientific consciousness.[13] According to James, all ideas must be interpreted in light of practical consequences, rather than purposes or metaphysical underpinnings.

There are no important differences in abstract truth that do not express themselves in concrete fact—no principles, absolutes, or *a prioris* can govern the pragmatic method, which is an attitude of casting one's glance away from first things toward last things, meaning the "fruits, consequences, facts" of life.[14]

It is indeed the very protean nature of pragmatism—its willingness to take in *anything*—combined with its democratic ethos and faith in scientific intelligence, that has made it an enduringly popular doctrine for Americans—politicians and jurists no less than private sector entrepreneurs. Indeed, in the pragmatic understanding, it seems any idea or pursuit can be justified, if it serves this ethos and this faith. The fact that versions of pragmatism are today espoused in all branches of American government—though they were not at the time of the Founding—is telling with respect to the development of our constitutional understandings.

Many have noted the movement in twentieth-century political rhetoric away from discussions of the Constitution or constitutionalism, and toward discussion of policy.[15] This move is at least partly a reflection of the hold of pragmatism on the American political imagination.

Dewey brought pragmatism and social Darwinism together as a compact set of political ideas, while showing their mutually reinforcing character. Dewey's pragmatism in some respects follows James's, but it remains reliant on the intellectual categories of "left" social Darwinism. James's purer pragmatism all but did away with the categories of nature and natural law that were still central, albeit only in a materialist sense, to the Darwinists.

Dewey's pragmatism, by contrast, reinjects natural forces and a strong sense of historical unfolding with which any method must comport itself. It is in Dewey that we can see how social Darwinism and pragmatism together become an intellectual and political force to be reckoned with: a modern liberalism whose goal is to help History—with a capital H—along its democratic path, relying on the intellectual inputs of an elite vanguard that need not directly consult the people or ask for their consent.

While still a graduate student at Johns Hopkins, Dewey had fortuitously heard the left social Darwinist Lester Frank Ward give his paper titled "Mind as a Social Factor."[16]

Dewey was deeply antagonistic—as was an increasing proportion of the intellectual class of his day—toward classical economics and philosophical individualism. Like Ward, Dewey conceived of human beings as having the capacity and responsibility for choices aimed at directing organic social and individual growth that is stifled by outmoded notions of competition and individual rights. Such choices and the policies that flow from them are always provisional responses to the flux of life, but their ultimate end is a more democratic society. Ideas grow and survive not because they are true or transcend human experience, but because they respond to it most effectively. "Social action" is called for once we understand that scientific intelligence can in fact superintend the unfolding of History.[17]

In his short book *Liberalism and Social Action*, based on a series of lectures, Dewey offers a history of liberalism, an analysis of the crisis it faces, and its prospects for a renaissance that will cement it as the guiding force of social life. As reason becomes purely instrumental, no longer concerned with ultimate truths but only "concrete situations,"[18] liberalism comes into its own. This new liberalism is far from its outmoded earlier version because it makes itself relevant to the problems of social organization and integration of various historically situated forces. In fact, the lack of a historical sense on the part of earlier liberals blinded them, according to Dewey, to the fact that their own interpretations of liberty were historically conditioned, rather than immutable truths.

Historical relativity finally frees liberalism to recognize economic relations are the "dominantly controlling" forces of modernity and that they require social control for the benefit of the many.[19] Free competition and removal of artificial barriers are no longer enough. Instead, the individual's powers must be "fed, sustained, and directed"[20] through cooperative control of the forces of production.[21] Individuality itself does not simply exist, but is attained through continuous growth.[22]

In Dewey we see a dominant theme of American progressivism and the New Deal, but also of twentieth-century liberalism more broadly: the belief that there is an intelligence, or "method of intelligence," that can be applied to solve social problems, which are themselves primarily economic in nature. It is this intelligence, which makes no pretence to knowledge except as a result of a pragmatic experimentation,[23] that captures the spirit of democracy more so than any philosophical or institutional analysis.

While all social relations are historically situated and in flux, there is one constant: the application of intelligence as a progressive ideal and method. "For the only adjustment that does not have to be made over again...is that effected through intelligence as a method,"[24] Dewey says. It is the only simulacrum of God in an otherwise desiccated world of process, evolution, and growth. Dewey rounds out his discussion by giving us insight into the nature of a "renascent liberalism." Growth must be physical, intellectual, and moral, and all classes and individuals must benefit. This of course means a vast state mechanism must be constructed that is confidently dedicated to ensuring growth, by means of progressive education, the welfare state, and redistribution of capital. The older political science of the Founding era, including that of *The Federalist*, is easily swept aside by Dewey. While the exact contours of public power and policy are not necessarily the same for him as they are for progressive political *actors* such as Theodore Roosevelt, Woodrow Wilson, or FDR, all agree that there are no inherent limits on state power.

Like the great progressive presidents, Dewey's political theory is impatient with constitutional restraints and institutional forms. Separation of powers is a doctrine rooted in stasis and therefore political death. Concerning oneself with constitutional forms and formalities is to give to institutions an abiding character they do not deserve. In Dewey one finds scant—or no—concern for such forms and formalities. Such considerations are subsumed to the newly political categories of change and growth. Long before "the courage to change" became an effective presidential campaign slogan, Dewey helped ensure "change" would have a central position in American political rhetoric. Dewey seems concerned about the exercise of arbitrary power, but has no concern for the aggregate power of the state. The cure for a powerful democratic state seems to be constant evolution in the direction of more democracy. The key to the perpetuation of our political institutions is far removed from either the constitutionalism of the Founders or the statesmanship of Lincoln.

In a telling encapsulation of social Darwinism, progressivism, and contemporary liberalism, Dewey claims, "[Flux] has to be controlled that it will move to some end in accordance with the principles of life, since life itself is development. Liberalism is committed to an end that is at once enduring and flexible: the liberation of individuals so that realization of their capacities may be the law of their life."[25] Human life therefore *is* nothing in particular, beyond a continual unfolding and advancement, and liberalism is dedicated to its liberation through social policy. When the economic necessities are provided, individuals may pursue the higher life according to their spiritual needs, whatever they might be, and however they might change. And change they will. Dewey's vision of liberalism is ultimately of an individual free of the various constraints that were previously thought by so many to be necessitated by a sometimes dangerous, and eternal, nature.

This vision of liberalism is a version of Marx's notion that truly free men may fish in the afternoon and criticize after dinner. Although today's constraints happen to be, for Dewey, largely economic in nature, it is not materialism but growth toward freedom that is at the heart of modern liberalism.

To conclude, as a consequence of the progressive synthesis—the melding of social Darwinism and pragmatism—the age-old question of "what works," politically—or what should be given a chance to prove itself—was increasingly divorced from a sense of constitutional restraint, as it was informed by an organic conception of a state un-limited in principle, whose only end was growth and development to buttress certain contemporary understandings of democracy and the choosing self.

By the early part of the twentieth century, the progressive synthesis began to bear real fruit. In the New Deal we see the first ripening of this fruit, in five different but overlapping guises:

1. the substitution of purported expertise for the invisible hand of the marketplace;
2. federal projects and, more significantly, *programs*;
3. the administrative state in all its manifestations;
4. the overcoming of federalism; and
5. the growth first of federal executive, and later judicial power.

All these were in the name of the superintendence of social and economic forces, to ensure that the "change" enlightened thinkers "hope" for—and believe at a deep level that History requires—is in fact the change we get.

In all of this, the Founders' Constitution could be relegated to an afterthought, to the extent it would be thought of at all. We have been bequeathed a very new deal, indeed.

Notes

Parts of this chapter are adapted from the author's book *Living Constitution, Dying Faith: Progressivism and the New Science of Jurisprudence* (Wilmington, DE: ISI Books, 2009).

1. Herman Belz, "The Constitution in the Gilded Age: The Beginnings of Constitutional Realism in American Scholarship," *The American Journal of Legal History* 13(2) (April 1969): 111.

2. Richard Hofstadter, *Social Darwinism in American Political Thought*, rev. ed. (Boston: Beacon Press, 1955). The phrase "social Darwinism" gained widespread intellectual currency as an appropriate descriptor of an amalgam of ideas only with the publication of the first edition of this book in 1944.

3. John Dewey, "The Influence of Darwinism on Philosophy," in *The Influence of Darwinism on Philosophy and Other Essays in Contemporary Thought* (New York: Henry Holt and Co., 1951).

4. The only other contender for the throne was the vigorous, pragmatic individualist frontier strain of thought associated with such figures as Frederick Jackson Turner and Mark Twain. But this strain was never as theoretically unified as social Darwinism, and never found the same acceptance among the intellectual classes. Not coincidentally, perhaps, it could not be said to have undermined, in any direct or consistent manner, the principled understanding of the American Founding articulated by Lincoln.

5. There are problems with this Deweyan tendency to identify nature as final cause or form with changelessness. Such an account comes close to capturing the essence of Plato's forms, but for Aristotle there are no fixed, immutable ideas separate from matter. Rather, things develop to their natural perfection, which for human beings is happiness, relying on a combination of intellectual and moral virtue. There is a tension in Aristotle between philosophy (man as knower) and politics (man being a political animal, i.e., a virtuous actor, rather than, or in addition to, a knower). It is far from clear, in either Aristotle or Plato, how these virtues interact at all levels. But what is clear is that there is no simple teleology in Aristotle when it comes to human beings. Simple teleologies are for the lower forms, whereas for humans there are choices involving politics, ethics, and philosophy, and nature many times misses its mark. Furthermore, for Aristotle, essence is not form simply, but activity or what a thing does. In his science, repose does not represent the highest state of being. Although there is a good amount of truth to Dewey's characterization of Western science, or philosophy, as the search for the transcendent, he seems wrong insofar as he puts a Platonic gloss on Aristotle.

6. Dewey, "The Influence of Darwinism on Philosophy," 13.

7. Ibid., 15.

8. Ibid., 16.

9. See, for example, John Dewey, *Reconstruction in Philosophy* (Boston: Beacon Press, 1957), *passim*.

10. This is the reason why we do not expect great statesmen—exercising practical and theoretical wisdom—to be young, whereas mathematicians might be.

11. Hofstadter, *Social Darwinism in American Thought*, 125.

12. William James, "What Pragmatism Means," in *Essays in Pragmatism*, ed. and intro. Alburey Castell (New York: Hafner Press, 1948); originally delivered by James as a lecture in 1906.

13. Ibid., 153–54.

14. Ibid., 146.

15. One need only compare the constitutional rhetoric of Lincoln to virtually any recent president to see this difference in stark relief. See Jeffrey K. Tulis, *The Rhetorical Presidency* (Princeton, NJ: Princeton University Press, 1987).

16. Louis Menand, *The Metaphysical Club: A Story of Ideas in America* (New York: Farrar, Straus, and Giroux, 2001), 302.

17. Indeed, Louis Menand notes that the growth of American social science disciplines was a consequence of the rejection of the notion that evolutionary laws govern in a way that cannot be improved upon by public policy. *See* ibid.

18. John Dewey, *Liberalism and Social Action* (Amherst, NY: Prometheus Books, 2000; orig. pub. 1935), 29.

19. Ibid., 42.

20. Ibid., 40.

21. Ibid., 59.

22. Ibid., 46.

23. Ibid., 80.

24. Ibid., 55–56.

25. Ibid., 61.

ALAN BRINKLEY

Legacies of the New Deal

The New Deal was controversial in its time, and it is controversial in the United States again today. It is credited by liberals with creating an effective and compassionate modern government. It is condemned by conservatives for starting the country down the road to a corrupting welfare state, an intrusive regulatory system, and an erosion in the autonomy of individuals and the market. It is considered by some to be a living, evolving force in American politics, and by others to be an obsolete relic of a repudiated past.

Here I will not discuss the origins of the New Deal or what it achieved—or failed to achieve—in the 1930s. Rather, I will examine its legacies and how the New Deal shapes our lives today.

The New Deal was a remarkably diverse set of efforts, reflecting the unusually eclectic ideologies of the people who worked in Franklin D. Roosevelt's government, and Roosevelt's willingness to tolerate a broad range of ideas. There were New Deal programs of great daring and originality, and New Deal programs of surprising clumsiness and lack of imagination; New Deal programs that were strikingly liberal, even radical, and New Deal programs that were highly conservative; New Deal programs that worked and New Deal programs that failed;

New Deal goals that were achieved, and New Deal goals that were never met (including the single most important goal—ending the Great Depression—which Roosevelt could never do until World War II did it for him). My purpose here is to differentiate between those aspects of the New Deal that shone brightly for a brief time and then disappeared without a trace—among them the National Recovery Administration (NRA), the Civilian Conservation Corps (CCC), and the Works Progress Administration (WPA)—and others that have left an enduring legacy in American life. There are several areas in which I believe the legacy of the New Deal remains visible today.

Politics

One legacy is political: the formation of a new and powerful national coalition of voters that made the Democratic Party—a weak minority party for nearly forty years before Roosevelt's election—into the dominant party in the United States for nearly forty years to come. The New Deal coalition, as it is known, no longer survives in anything like the form it assumed in the 1930s, and the Democratic Party no longer has the extraordinary dominance it had from the 1930s to the 1960s; but significant elements of that coalition remain important to American political life.

The New Deal made the Democratic Party the preferred party for people of liberal or progressive or leftist inclinations in the United States, many of whom had previously considered the Republican Party, the party of Theodore Roosevelt and many other reformers, more reliably progressive. This broad coalition of progressives has remained a core constituency of the Democratic Party ever since.

The New Deal also helped to create a strong and enduring alliance between the Democratic Party and organized labor (which owed much of its economic strength to New Deal labor legislation). Both the power of unions, and their ability to shape their members' political views, has declined significantly since then, but the alliance with labor organizations survives as a distinctive and important part of the Democratic Party.

The New Deal made the Democratic Party the party of African-Americans and most other minorities. Black Americans had been mostly

Republican in the first seventy years after the Civil War, a tribute to Lincoln and his party's connection with the abolition of slavery, but Roosevelt made them Democrats. That was not because the New Deal committed itself to the struggle among African-Americans for civil rights, which was already slowly taking root in the social landscape of the 1930s. On the contrary, the Roosevelt administration was notably timid about civil rights issues. But the New Deal did provide African-Americans with desperately needed social services and at times, at least, suggested a greater sympathy for their larger aspirations for equality than had most previous presidents. By 1936, over 90 percent of black American voters were voting for Roosevelt and the Democrats.

Together, these changes in the Democratic Party's constituency (along with its subsequent loss of some of its more conservative groups, most notably the withdrawal of white southerners from the party beginning in the 1960s) contributed to making the Democratic Party consistently the more progressive of the two parties. That remains true today, despite the continuing and successful efforts of many Democrats to move the party more to the center.

The Physical Landscape

The New Deal left an enduring legacy to modern America by transforming parts of the nation's physical landscape. The New Deal was among the most expansive and ambitious episodes in the construction of public works of any period in American history. The 1930s was a period of great public works building in much of the industrial world, particularly in nations where strong governments were attempting both to make progress against the Depression and create a physical image of and monument to themselves. In this respect, New Deal America had something in common with Germany, Italy, and the Soviet Union in the 1930s.

The physical legacy of the New Deal is visible in almost every community in the United States, in schools and post offices and government office buildings built by the Works Progress Administration, and in the striking murals with which the Treasury and the WPA arts project adorned many of them. It is visible in the first major public housing projects in American history, and in a vast range of massive infrastructure projects—bridges, highways, harbors, dams and other hydroelectric projects. This helped transform the economic future of previously underdeveloped areas of the South and West, in preparation for the great postwar development that changed them into the prosperous, developed region now known as the Sunbelt, the fastest growing area of the United States. The New Deal's legacy is visible in its connection of countless once-isolated rural people to the modern world through electrification projects—especially the Rural Electrification Administration (REA)—that made it possible for them to begin living as most other twentieth-century Americans lived. Some historians have argued that the "public investment" or "state capitalism" of the New Deal was the principal goal of some of the most important New Dealers and that it was the source of Roosevelt's single most important legacy.

The Welfare State

Almost certainly the most conspicuous (and controversial) legacy of the New Deal is its contribution to the creation of the modern American welfare state. Those contributions took several forms.

In the 1930s, the New Deal was perhaps best known to unemployed Americans for its vast work relief programs, through which the government created paying jobs—many of them through the public works programs—to get men (and some women) back to work and so help families survive the crisis. Work relief was an appealing temporary solution to the problem of unemployment because it addressed a clear and compelling need, and did so in a way that seemed to preserve the principle that relief should be earned, that no one should receive something for nothing. Virtually none of the New Deal's relief programs survived World War II, largely because the war produced so much demand for labor that it was no longer necessary for the government to create jobs. The experience of work relief did have one important, lasting impact. It created a precedent for the still powerful assumption among most Americans that the government should assist them when they are in trouble. And although the government has not always responded effectively to those expectations, the expectation survives.

The more enduring institutional contributions of the New Deal to the creation of the modern welfare state fall into two categories. One was the wide range of new programs and protections that have helped mostly middle-class people: mortgage protection for homes and small farms; insurance of personal bank deposits; income tax deductions for interest on home mortgages; and many other economic benefits and protections that have provided increased security and opportunity. The other is the equally wide range of programs that have established the basic structure of the formal welfare state of the remainder of the twentieth century: unemployment insurance; pensions for the elderly; aid to the disabled; and, perhaps the most controversial, assistance to single mothers with children—all are products of the Social Security Act of 1935, the single most important piece of social welfare legislation in American history.

The New Deal welfare state created much of the social protection Americans presently receive. Some of those programs remain very successful, most notably unemployment insurance, which has removed much of the desperation from the lives of men and women temporarily laid off from work, and old age pensions, which have lifted millions of elderly Americans out of poverty and remaking them as a group from being the poorest Americans to among the most affluent. But the New Deal also built into its welfare programs the longstanding distinction between the "deserving" and the "undeserving poor," which led to the provision of relatively generous benefits to those who could be said to have earned them or paid for them (veterans, for example, and workers and old people, who had made contributions to insurance programs) and much less generous benefits to those who simply "needed" them, most notably single women with children, whose benefits were never large and which were always accompanied by intrusive screening requirements. (Since 1996, of course, the federal welfare program has moved in a very different direction—with benefits aimed at those who work more than at those who do not, thus helping to link the welfare system to the New Deal's earlier preoccupation with workfare. This has served to reduce the controversies surrounding welfare.)

Economic Reform

In the beginning at least, most New Dealers believed that their principle responsibility—other than the one that defined all others, namely ending the Great Depression—was to reform American capitalism. Indeed, nothing was so critical to the belief system of the early New Deal than that something was wrong with capitalism and that it was government's responsibility to fix it.

Those efforts at economic reform were not always successful. Some—for example, the National Recovery Act of 1933, perhaps the most ambitious program the New Deal created—were disastrous failures. But the accumulated result of New Deal economic initiatives, although very different from what early New Dealers had wanted or expected, was nevertheless a significantly, although far from radically, reformed capitalism, and a substantial expansion of the role of government in guiding it.

The enduring institutional changes in the nature of capitalism are easy to identify. The New Deal's Agricultural Adjustment Act and succeeding farm legislation gave American farmers a range of new protections against the instability of the agricultural market, protections for which many farmers had been clamoring for a generation or more. There were significant flaws in the AAA, both in its impact on the economy as a whole and on the lives of farmers. But its system of subsidies, price supports, and production restrictions did help raise farm prices and keep the agricultural economy from collapsing. Those programs have survived, even though in a changed and now much diminished form, into our own time. New Deal labor legislation, both Section 7a of the 1933 National Industrial Recovery Act and the much more important National Labor Relations Act of 1935 (better known as the Wagner Act), established organized labor as a powerful and protected force within the industrial economy, able to bargain collectively with employers who had previously refused to negotiate with them and to play an enduring role in the distribution of resources and political power in the industrial world. The political mobilization of farmers and workers, and the creation of institutions that codified their rights and powers, was one of the most important New Deal contributions to political economy. It helped make

American capitalism more pluralistic than it had been in the past. It created a more contested marketplace, one in which capitalists not only had to compete with one another but now also had to bargain, and even compete, with workers and farmers in ways they had never been required to before. As a result, the modern American political economy is often described as a "broker state," a value-neutral setting in which different groups compete for favors and advancement.

The New Deal also expanded considerably the system of public regulation of private authority that earlier periods of reform had begun. It created the Securities and Exchange Commission, which for the first time provided for government oversight and regulation of the stock markets and which helped reduce the recklessness and fraud that had helped produce the catastrophic market collapse of 1929. It created the Federal Aviation Administration, the Federal Communications Commission, and other agencies to regulate economic activities that made use of such public properties as the airwaves and the skies. It increased, if tentatively and intermittently, the government's attention to monopolistic combinations and to corporate behavior in restraint of trade by aggressively pursuing antitrust measures. It significantly increased the power of the Federal Reserve Board to regulate banking practices, and it stabilized American banks through a reinvigorated system of regulation and a new system of deposit insurance. This last item, of course, proved to be of extraordinary importance in our current economic crisis.

In the late years of the New Deal, in the aftermath of a serious recession in 1937–1938 and in response to the obstinacy of a depression that five years of New Deal efforts had failed to end, Roosevelt began experimenting with other approaches to economic policy—most notably with what was coming to be known as Keynesian economics. An ill-advised effort to balance the budget by cutting government spending had appeared to precipitate the disastrous 1937–1938 recession. A vigorous new program of spending and investment launched in early 1938 helped bring the economy back to at least limited life. Out of that partial success emerged the growing belief that government could influence the economy through its monetary and fiscal policies, through its control over the money supply and its ability to raise and lower spending and taxation.

To many younger New Dealers, the discovery of the power of these fiscal and monetary instruments was a revelation. No longer would it be necessary to search for ways to reform capitalist institutions in order to revive the economy and produce economic growth. Even unreformed institutions could be helped to work better through the intelligent application of fiscal and monetary policies. It was, they now believed, possible to manage capitalism without managing the institutions of capitalism, to help the economy revive without engaging in the politically and bureaucratically difficult effort to force capitalists to change their behavior or restructure their corporations. To the most exuberant Keynesians, this discovery meant that the greatest dilemma of the modern industrial world had been resolved, that the problem of monopoly—the problem that had preoccupied and frustrated more than two generations of reform efforts—need no longer preoccupy modern society; that it would be possible to lead the way to economic growth not by focusing on producers but by helping consumers, by pumping money into the hands of the millions of men and women who created the markets for what capitalists produced.

The New Deal never fully embraced the Keynesian Revolution, and indeed no subsequent American government ever fully embraced it either. In recent years, fiscal policy as an instrument of economic management has been discredited by deficits and by the increasingly global character of the economy, and monetary policy has replaced it as the centerpiece of government intervention in the economy—although Keynesianism has had a significant, if perhaps brief, revival with the enormous stimulus package the Obama administration enacted early in 2009. But however differently from its intentions, the New Deal did help create the belief that government not only had a responsibility to create or sustain prosperity, but that it could do so without intruding too directly into the affairs of the capitalist world.

Presidential Leadership

No evaluation of the legacy of the New Deal would be complete without attention to the legacy of Franklin Roosevelt himself and to the impact of his leadership on his successors and on leaders around the world.

There is some irony in this. Roosevelt himself was not always the power-ful, committed figure he appeared to be. He was, unbeknownst to the vast majority of Americans at the time, paralyzed from the waist down, unable to walk without the assistance of an elaborate system of braces, crutches, and canes, and mostly confined to a wheelchair. During the last years of his life—and of his presidency—he was desperately ill, his condition concealed from all but a few.

Roosevelt was a leader with few strong convictions or principles. He "was content in large measure to follow public opinion," the histo-rian Richard Hofstadter once wrote, and thus charted no clear path.[1] He allowed the existing political landscape to dictate his course, the historian James MacGregor Burns lamented, instead of reshaping the Democratic Party to serve his own purposes.[2] Such complaints were common among Roosevelt's contemporaries as well, most of all among those who had invested the greatest hopes in him: his eagerness to please everyone with whom he spoke, his ability to persuade people expressing opposing views that he agreed with them both, his tendency to allow seemingly contradictory initiatives to proceed simultaneously. "When I talk to him, he says 'Fine! Fine! Fine!,'" Senator Huey Long of Louisiana once complained. "But Joe Robinson [the Senate major-ity leader and one of Long's ideological nemeses] goes to see him the next day and again he says 'Fine! Fine! Fine!' Maybe he says 'Fine' to everybody."[3] Henry Stimson, Roosevelt's Secretary of War from 1940 on, was constantly frustrated by this enigmatic man. Not long after Roosevelt died, Stimson privately expressed relief that in Harry Truman, the new president, he finally had someone willing to make a clear-cut and unequivocal decision.[4] Roosevelt's fundamentally political nature, and his inclination to measure each decision against its likely popular reaction, may have been a significant weakness, as some of his critics have claimed, or his greatest strength, as others insist. But it was the essence of the man.

Roosevelt believed in capitalism, as all but a few Americans did. He also believed that government had a positive obligation to save it from its difficulties, and that among the things necessary to save it was assistance to the victims of its collapse. But he had few deep commit-ments beyond that, and was instead—to the frequent frustration of more principled people around him—endlessly flexible, always compromising, frequently dissembling, never fully trustworthy or loyal to those with whom he worked.

But Roosevelt was a great leader despite, and perhaps even because of, these apparent weaknesses. His paralysis from polio, which was surely one of the most important aspects of his life from the early 1920s until his death, gave him much of the steely determination that made him president and that allowed him to survive four national campaigns. It also gave him much of his public demeanor of sunny, garrulous optimism. Roosevelt, like many disabled people, went to great lengths to distract people from his disability by being conspicuously cheerful and self-confident, an image he skillfully conveyed not just to those around him but to the entire nation and the world. Whatever the reasons, Roosevelt presented himself as a beacon of confidence and optimism, and considering the panicked environment in which he entered office that alone was a significant achievement. The firm, confident voice, the smiling optimism, the cock of the head, the up-tilted cigarette holder, the beaming smile all helped many desperate people to believe that there was hope in their leadership, that the head of their nation was not just a bureaucrat but a symbol of their highest aspirations. That image has survived for over sixty years as a potent model of presidential leadership to many Americans.

Roosevelt's ideological flexibility, frustrating as it may have been to those around him, was in fact one of his greatest strengths as a leader. It was responsible for one of the New Deal's most conspicuous and, in my opinion, most valuable features: its commitment to pragmatic experimentation. Roosevelt inherited a political world constricted in countless ways by fervently held principles on both the left and the right. Conservatives hewed on principle to the gold standard, to a balanced budget, to the sanctity of private contracts, to the obligation to protect capital whatever the cost, and above all to the belief that the invisible hand of the market must be permitted to govern the affairs of society without interference from the visible hand of the state. Some on the left embraced hostility to capitalism itself and an insistence on punishing the wealthy. Into that ideologically constricted world Roosevelt introduced a willingness to consider striking innovations, to cast aside deeply held inhibitions, to treat beliefs not as fixed and inviolable principles but as things to be tested and, if necessary, revised or repudiated. There were, of course, many things he would not do, some principles he would not abandon, some important new ideas he was slow to embrace or to which he was always resistant. But much of what was important about the New Deal was a result of the degree to which Roosevelt was open to what he liked to call the "spirit of persistent experimentation."

Critics and admirers alike have argued that the New Deal reflected nothing but pragmatic responses to immediate problems, that it was, as Hofstadter described, little more than a "chaos of experimentation."[5] "To look upon these programs as the result of a unified plan," Roosevelt's erstwhile advisor Raymond Moley wrote in a sour memoir published after his falling out with the president, "was to believe that the accumulation of stuffed snakes, baseball pictures, school flags, old tennis shoes, carpenter's tools, geometry books, and chemistry sets in a boy's bedroom could have been put there by an interior decorator."[6] But it also reflected Roosevelt's instinct for action: his belief in, if nothing else, the obligation of the leaders of government to work aggressively and affirmatively to deal with the nation's problems. "Take a method and try it," Roosevelt liked to say. "If it fails, admit it frankly and try another. But above all, try something." In a rapidly changing world of increasing uncertainty and complexity, there is much to be said, I believe, for the legacy of ideological flexibility and spirited experimentation that the New Deal bequeathed to American public life.

Notes

1. Richard Hofstadter, *The Age of Reform* (New York: Alfred A. Knopf, 1955), 412.
2. James MacGregor Burns, *Roosevelt: The Lion and the Fox* (New York: Harvest Books, 1956).
3. William E. Leuchtenburg, *The FDR Years: On Roosevelt and His Legacy* (New York: Columbia University Press, 1995), 78.
4. Henry L. Stimson and McGeorge Bundy, *On Active Service in Peace and War* (New York: Octagon Books, 1971), 256–325.
5. Hofstadter, *Age of Reform*, 307.
6. David Kennedy, *Freedom from Fear: The American People in Depression and War, 1929–1945* (New York: Oxford University Press, 1999), 154.

BURTON FOLSOM, JR.

Keynesianism and the Economic Principles of the New Deal

When we talk about the Great Depression, one point we need to establish at the outset is that the government was heavily responsible for creating the conditions that created the Great Depression. Other essays in this volume discuss the problems of the Federal Reserve: Rising interest rates and the disappearance of one-fourth to one-third of our money supply were very damaging. Milton Friedman won the Nobel Prize largely for his work on the Great Depression and the Federal Reserve.

Another problem was the Smoot–Hawley Tariff, which was passed in 1930 and had a critical negative impact. This tariff raised prices on over a thousand items, and there were significant tariffs on 3,200 items. For example, the Swiss sell us a watch, its major export, for about $2. We then add a $2 tariff onto the cost, so that American consumers have to pay $4 for a $2 watch. The result is that not many Swiss watches are sold, inhibiting our export/import market. Switzerland then enacts retaliatory tariffs and the Swiss, in turn, refuse to buy our products. The U.S. auto industry, for example, sold 5 million cars in 1929; in 1933 that was down to 1.5 million.

Then Herbert Hoover proceeded to enact—with the cooperation of Congress, of course—the highest peace-time taxes in U.S. history:

income taxes, and excise taxes. This led investors to retreat from making investments that would have bolstered the economy, and to put their money into tax-exempt bonds and foreign investments. Consequently, the economy contracted, which led to the unemployment rate of 25 percent that we had in 1932 and 1933.

The second point that needs to be made is that the government's attempt to remedy the Depression—that attempt being the New Deal—was a failure. I say that based on using unemployment rates as a measure of success. Until the time of the Great Depression, the United States had never experienced unemployment higher than 17 percent. In April 1939, toward the end of Franklin D. Roosevelt's second term, unemployment was 20.7%. Ten years after the Great Depression had started, unemployment was four points higher than at any time before the 1930s. What an absolute disaster.

I began my book *New Deal or Raw Deal* with a quotation from FDR's Secretary of Treasury, Henry Morgenthau. He and Roosevelt had been friends for decades. (Eleanor Roosevelt once said that Henry Morgenthau was one of two people who could tell FDR that he was wrong and get away with it.) Despite this personal closeness, Morgenthau made this commentary on the New Deal in 1939, right after unemployment had reached almost 21 percent: "We have tried spending money, we are spending more than we have ever spent before and it does not work, and I have just one interest, and if I am wrong, somebody else can have my job. I want to see this country prosperous, I want to see people get a job, I want to see people get enough to eat. We have never made good on our promises. I say after eight years of this administration, we have just as much unemployment as when we started and enormous debt to boot."[1] All of this is true. The national debt had doubled at that point, seven years into the FDR administration. By these measures, the New Deal was a colossal failure.

This suggests that government solutions do not work well. It suggests that the ideas of John Maynard Keynes do not work well. Keynes had come to the conclusion that we needed to spend a lot of money on public works to ease the effects of the Depression. Called Aggregate Demand Management, the idea is that increased government spending will have a multiplier effect, which, eventually, will remedy the situation.

Of course, in order to obtain the money it will spend, the government has to increase taxes or go into debt.

And this is what Keynes seems to be saying. I say "seems" because if you read Keynes, you quickly learn that there is Keynesian English and there is English English. See, for example, this quote from his *General Theory of Employment, Interest, and Money*: "Men are involuntarily unemployed if in the event of a small rise in the price of wage goods, relative to the money wage, both the aggregate supply of labor willing to work for the current money wage, and the aggregate demand for it, at that wage, would be greater than the existing volume of unemployment."[2] There you have it.

The interpretation that was given to his writings was that we needed to invest, and invest heavily, in public works. Keynes himself said that "if we pulled all the houses down in South London and then rebuilt them, that would put lots of people to work."[3] But Keynes wasn't the only one who held these views. They were in the air, part of the progressive impulse of the 1930s, which had evolved from the early 1900s. Let's examine some of the resultant programs.

The Agricultural Adjustment Act (AAA) was instituted to curb overproduction of farm products and to increase farmers' low incomes. The government would pay farmers not to produce, provided they took part of their land out of production. The AAA also included a parity system to help raise the price of their crops, but its fundamental concept was that paying farmers not to farm would alleviate the farm crisis.

This particular program was the brainchild of Professor John D. Black, an economist at Harvard. It was such a wonderful idea—and interesting because of its progressive impulse, the optimism that we can solve the problems of humankind.

In exchange for taking one-quarter of their land out of production, the government would pay farmers roughly $10 per acre (about $100 an acre today). While farmers would agree not to farm a portion of their land, not all of them kept their promises. To discourage this dishonesty, the government would send inspectors out to measure farmland and to make sure one-fourth was not being used. Some farmers would then bribe the inspectors, which made it necessary to send inspectors to inspect the inspectors! And just in case that wasn't enough, aerial surveillance was added to the mix.

In 1933, farmers were paid not to farm, and two years later there were crop shortages. In 1935, the United States had to import 34 million bushels of corn, 13 million bushels of wheat, and 36 million pounds of cotton. True, the weather was a contributing factor, and the crop yield was poor that year, but nonetheless—the government had paid farmers not to produce, and then had to turnaround and pay high prices for imports.

The National Industrial Recovery Act (NIRA), discussed elsewhere in this volume, was another disaster. The government told businessmen to set the prices for their products and the government would make those prices legally binding. The result was that people went to jail for offering discounts to their customers. Jacob Maged's tailor shop in Jersey City, New Jersey, was not located on the main shopping street. To encourage people to walk the extra distance to his shop, Mr. Maged decided to charge 35 cents to press a pair of pants, not the NIRA-enforced price of 40 cents. The NIRA closed him down and sent him to jail. The *Washington Post* wrote: "It didn't matter if Maged had to charge less than the bright shiny tailor shop up the street if he wanted to continue to exist. The law said he couldn't."[4] The *New York Herald Tribune* wrote, "For a parallel it is necessary to go to the fascist or communist states of Europe."[5] In 1935 the Supreme Court struck down the NIRA.

The big pump-priming act of the New Deal was the WPA, the Works Progress Administration. Its charge was to build roads, bridges, airports, and schools. Again, this sounds good in theory: Put the unemployed to work building infrastructure. The WPA was funded by $4.8 billion dollars, and at that time was the largest domestic program in American history. However, Roosevelt had tremendous control over the allocation of these funds. The result was he divvied up the money based on political expediency, which means this incredible program subsidized much of the New Deal. V. G. Copeland, the Democratic County Chairman of Indiana, captured the essence of the New Deal: "What I think will help, is to change the WPA management from top to bottom. Put men in there who are in favor of using these Democratic projects to make votes for the Democratic party."[6] James Doherty, a

New Hampshire Democrat, agreed: "It is my personal belief that to the victor belongs the spoils and that Democrats should be holding most of those WPA positions so that we might strengthen our fences for the 1940 election."[7] One WPA Director in New Jersey, a corrupt but candid man, answered his telephone: "Democratic Headquarters."

There is a huge file in the National Archives labeled "WPA/ Political Corruption." In it you can find some real gems. For example, Congressman Frank Towey announced at a Democratic rally in Newark, New Jersey: "In this county there are 18,000 people on the WPA with an average of three people in a family, you have 54,000 potential Democratic votes. Can anyone beat that if it is properly mobilized?"[8] This is how Franklin Roosevelt won elections—and he won them big.

When asked about FDR's failures, his defenders have a fallback position: "Well, yes," they say, "but he must have given people hope. FDR did have his fireside chats, which were very popular. He did give people hope—and jobs. He was trying, he was doing his best, and you have to give him credit for that."

But the Founders were specific in Article One, Section Eight of the Constitution about not letting programs such as these be part of the federal government. Such federalization put a huge political war chest into the hands of the president. Even FDR's friends agreed that this was happening. Carter Glass, the Democratic senator from Virginia, said: "The 1936 elections would have been much closer had my party not had a four billion eight hundred million dollar relief bill as campaign fodder." Pennsylvania is a good example. Because it was a very important swing state that the Democrats had not carried in decades, a lot of WPA money was directed to Pennsylvania. Then Democrats running for office there could say, "If you would like this to continue, vote for Roosevelt and vote the Democratic ticket." As one Republican said after the election, "Apparently you can't beat Santa Claus."[9]

Many New Deal programs, prominent at that time, are rarely mentioned any more. The Silver Purchase Act, for example, paid miners 64.5 cents an ounce for silver when the market price was around 40 cents an ounce. Again this amounted to a subsidy to six western states, an exchange for votes (which Roosevelt got). But the law of unintended consequences kicked in and there was a huge increase in the amount of silver produced. Some of it had been smuggled across the border from Mexico, where it had been purchased for 40 cents an ounce. According to the rules of the Silver Purchase Act, the silver had to be stockpiled; after eight years of stockpiling, the government had 42,000 tons of silver. This represented almost two percent of the national debt—but it could not be cashed in. There was no silver lining in that cloud.

During World War II the government finally did spend the silver—it had to for the war industry—and Roosevelt worried that he wouldn't be able to continue to carry those western states. This is where things began to get tragic. Once power is centralized and increased in the state, we get unfortunate occurrences, such as the rounding up of Japanese-Americans during World War II. This was very popular with many of the same people who were angry because the government was using their silver. Eric L. Muller, in *American Inquisition: The Hunt for Japanese American Disloyalty in World War II* (Chapel Hill: The University of North Carolina Press, 2007), documents how Roosevelt knew in 1942–1943 that the Japanese were loyal, many fighting overseas in a very loyal way for the United States. But he would not release them from the internment camps because that would upset the western states—and the 1944 election, in which he planned to run for a fourth term, was coming up. And that became a reason for their continued internment.

It is impossible to ignore the politics of all of this, the politics of federal programs, centralizing power, the use of those programs to, in effect, bribe or buy votes to win a reelection and change American politics forever. Poor Alf Landon, who was running against Roosevelt, said, "Oh this triple A is terrible." And then Roosevelt said, "Well, what are you going to do?" A lot of farmers said, "You're going to take our subsidy away?" "Uh, no, no I won't take your subsidy away," Landon said, "I'll manage it better." So the choice in 1936 was voting for the guy who gave you your subsidy, or for the guy who alleges he will manage your subsidy better. How to respond to that has been the Republican Party's dilemma ever since.

These programs have to be paid for with taxes, but you almost never see a book on the New Deal that discusses taxes—and that subject has to be discussed. We had very high taxes on the wealthy during those years. Roosevelt raised the top rate of the federal income tax to

79 percent in 1935. In other words, the government was asking investors to give up four-fifths of their income beyond a certain level, money that could have been invested in companies. When the wealthy protested, Roosevelt became angry and built his 1936 campaign against them. "They hate me," FDR said, "and I welcome their hatred."[10]

In 1937 Roosevelt cut spending. The cut was slight and the deficit was still large, but spending is always cut slightly after an election. Roosevelt had just been reelected so the WPA employment numbers dropped because he didn't need those people anymore. We also had something that is not often mentioned: an undistributed profits tax—a special tax—on corporations. Roosevelt encouraged, to some extent, mandatory collective bargaining, which resulted in the unionization of the auto companies. The minimum wage law passed, which is with us today and which continues to prevent employers from hiring people, which continues to increase unemployment.

Then FDR turned the IRS loose. He turned it against Andrew Mellon and he turned it against Moses Annenberg. Moses Annenberg edited the *Philadelphia Inquirer*, which ran editorials condemning Roosevelt. An IRS investigation ensued, Annenberg owed money and he went to prison. Then we find that the editor of the *Philadelphia Record*, a Democratic paper, received help from the Reconstruction Finance Corporation in securing a loan.

In 1938 and 1939, Roosevelt said to Morgenthau, "We need to go after all of these rich people with an IRS investigation." Morgenthau said, "Well, wait a minute here, why do we do that?" and Roosevelt said, "Because it can gain us ten million votes."[11] We condemn the rich, we blame them for not hiring people. Then when they don't hire, we can blame them, and that justifies starting a public works program from the taxes that we are taking from them, which prevents them from expanding their factories.

This raises the question, What ended the Great Depression? I don't want to pretend we have absolute answers—research is ongoing. But you can't very well end a depression by building an army, making weapons, and bombing others. That is not getting us out of the Great Depression. When World War II began, 12 million people were sent overseas, and 12 to 15 million people were put to work stateside in the defense industry. As a result, unemployment went way down. (For a while the WPA continued operations as well because Roosevelt still had elections to win.) But the national debt during the war went from $40 billion to $260 billion, a sixfold increase. We traded unemployment for debt.

So the war didn't solve the Great Depression, and now the issue is what are we going to do when the boys come home? Many New Dealers said we need a new New Deal. They called it the New Deal Revival, a host of new federal programs, but they were not successful. Senator Walter George, on October 24, 1945, supported a bill to cut tax rates to get us out of the Great Depression: "You're right, the Great Depression is going to go on after the war if we continue the New Deal," George said. Instead we need tax cuts because that is what we tried in the 1920s, when the top rate was 25 percent. That is what worked then.

In the 1920s Andrew Mellon, then Secretary of the Treasury, said: "It seems difficult for some to understand that high rates of taxation do not necessarily mean large revenue to the government and that more revenue may often be obtained by lower rates."[12] In other words, he is saying that if you cut rates, in addition to encouraging investment, it may actually increase revenue. He was right on both counts. Calvin Coolidge had the lowest inflation and unemployment rate of any president of the twentieth century. We had budget surpluses every year of the 1920s. We chopped almost one-third off the national debt.

After World War II, the income tax rate was 94 percent on all income over $200,000, and the top corporate rate was 90 percent. Senator George's bill was going to lower the income tax rate some, but it was going to lower the corporate rate a lot, by removing the excess profits tax and cutting that 90 percent rate down to 38 percent. Senator Walter George said: "This bill is properly a tax rate reducing bill. It will not necessarily reduce the amount of revenue coming in. Indeed, if it has the effect which it is hoped it will have, it will so stimulate the expansion of business as it to bring in a greater total revenue."[13]

Senator Albert Hawkes, a former businessman from New Jersey, said: "The repeal of the Excess Profits Tax, in my opinion, may raise more revenue for the United States than would be raised if it were retained."[14] Those bills were passed and over a period of three to four years we see a sharp increase in revenue to the government. But more than that, the bills sent a message to businesspeople that by cutting your taxes, we want you to invest again in the American economy. And they did invest—in tremendous amounts—and we had only 3.9% unemployment in 1946 and 1947. The tax cuts, I think, played a big role in getting us out of the Great Depression.

I regret that the New Deal was an abysmal failure. It sent us in the wrong direction, but we were able to overcome parts of it. That the tax cuts produced more economic growth is a remarkable example of that. President Kennedy in the 1960s and President Reagan in the 1980s both cut tax rates and both saw tremendous economic growth and a lowering of unemployment. I would like to suggest that our country avoid stimulus packages, priming the pump with WPAs, and Keynesian arguments that vast public works will help us out of our current situation. Instead let's cut tax rates and not allow central planners and presidents to determine which politically good districts to send the money into. Let business people and the American people invest, start up businesses, expand existing ones, and put people to work. We developed television, copiers, and rock music after the war, and sent the American economy on a prosperous route with relative freedom and limited government.

Notes

1. Morgenthau Diary, May 9, 1939, in Franklin D. Roosevelt Presidential Library.
2. Mark Skousen, *The Making of Modern Economics* (London: Me. E. Sharpe, 2001), 332.
3. Ibid., 341.
4. *Washington Post*, April 22, 1934.
5. *New York Herald-Tribune*, April 23, 1934.
6. James Patterson, *The New Deal and the States* (Princeton, NJ: Princeton University Press, 1969), 82–83.
7. Ibid.
8. *Newark Evening News*, September 8, 1938.
9. Burton Folsom, Jr., *New Deal or Raw Deal?* (New York: Simon & Schuster, 2008), 171–76.
10. Gary Dean Best, *Pride, Prejudice, and Politics* (Westport, CT: Prager, 1991), 136.
11. Folsom, *New Deal or Raw Deal?*, 166.

12. Burton Folsom, Jr., *The Myth of the Robber Barons* (Herndon, VA: Young America's Foundation, 2009), 103.

13. Burton Folsom, Jr., and Anita Folsom, "Did FDR End the Great Depression? *Wall Street Journal*, April 12, 2010.

14. Ibid.

AMITY SHLAES

The Rules of the Game and Economic Recovery

The *Monopoly* board game originated during the Great Depression. At first its inventor, Charles Darrow, could not interest manufacturers. Parker Brothers turned the game down, citing "52 design errors." But Darrow produced his own copies of the game, and Parker Brothers finally bought *Monopoly*. By 1935, the *New York Times* was reporting that "leading all other board games... is the season's craze, 'Monopoly,' the game of real estate."[1]

Most of us are familiar with the object of *Monopoly*: the accumulation of property on which one places houses and hotels, and from which one receives revenue. Many of us have a favorite token. Perennially popular is the top hat, which symbolizes the sort of wealth to which Americans who work hard can aspire. The top hat is a token that has remained in the game, even while others have changed over the decades.

One's willingness to play *Monopoly* depends on a few conditions—for instance, a predictable number of "Pay Income Tax" cards. These cards are manageable when you know in advance the amount of money printed on them and how many of them are in the deck. It helps, too,

---

A version of this essay was delivered as the Manhattan Institute's 2009 Hayek Prize lecture.

that there are a limited and predictable number of "Go to Jail" cards. This is what Frank Knight of the University of Chicago would call a knowable risk, as opposed to an uncertainty. Likewise, there must be a limited and predictable number of "Chance" cards. In other words, there has to be some certainty that property rights are secure and that the risks to property are few in number and can be managed.

The bank must be dependable, too. There is a fixed supply of *Monopoly* money and the bank is supposed to follow the rules of the game, exercising little or no independent discretion. If players sit down at the *Monopoly* board only to discover a bank that overreaches or is too unpredictable or discretionary, we all know what happens. They will walk away from the board. There is no game.

Relevance to the 1930s

How is this game relevant to the Great Depression? We all know the traditional narrative of that event: The stock market crash generated an economic Katrina. One in four was unemployed in the first few years. It resulted from a combination of monetary, banking, credit, international, and consumer confidence factors. The terrible thing about it was the duration of a high level of unemployment, which averaged in the mid-teens for the entire decade.

Another thing we usually learn is that the Depression was mysterious—a problem that only experts with doctorates could solve. That is why FDR's floating advisory group—Felix Frankfurter, Frances Perkins, George Warren, Marriner Eccles, and Adolf Berle, among others—was sometimes known as the Brains Trust. The mystery had something to do with a shortage of money, we are told, and in the end, only a brain trust's tinkering with the money supply saved us. The corollary to this view is that the government knows more than American business does about economics.

Another common presumption is that cleaning up Wall Street and getting rid of white-collar criminals helped the nation recover. And although property rights still may have mattered during the 1930s, they mattered less than government-created jobs, shoring up homeowners, and getting the money supply right. American democracy, it was believed, was threatened by the rise of a potential plutocracy, and that the Wagner Act of 1935—which lent federal support to labor unions—was thus necessary and proper. Finally, the traditional view of the 1930s is that action by the government was good, whereas inaction would have been fatal. The economic crisis mandated any kind of action, no matter how far removed it might be from sound monetary policy. Along these lines the humorist Will Rogers wrote in 1933 that if Franklin Roosevelt had "burned down the capital, we would cheer and say, 'Well at least we got a fire started, anyhow.'"[2]

To put this official version of the 1930s in terms of the *Monopoly* board: The American economy was failing because there were too many top hats lording it about on the board, trying to establish a plutocracy, and because there was no bank to hand out money. Under FDR, the federal government became the bank and pulled America back to economic health.

When you go to research the 1930s, however, you find a different story. It is of course true that the early part of the Depression—the years upon which most economists have focused—was an economic Katrina. And a number of New Deal measures provided lasting benefits for the economy. These include the creation of the Securities and Exchange Commission, the push for free trade led by Secretary of State Cordell Hull, and the establishment of the modern mortgage format. But the remaining evidence contradicts the official narrative. Overall, it can be said, government prevented recovery. Herbert Hoover was too active, not too passive—as the old stereotypes suggest—while Roosevelt and his New Deal policies impeded recovery as well, especially during the latter half of the decade.

In short, the prolonged Depression can be put down to government arrogance—arrogance that came at the expense of economic common sense, the rule of law, and respect for property rights.

Arrogance and Discretion

Consider the centerpiece of the New Deal's first 100 days, the National Recovery Administration (NRA), which was in effect an enormous multisector mechanism calibrated to manage the business cycle

through industrial codes that, among other things, regulated prices.
The principles on which its codes were based appear risible from the
perspective of microeconomics and common sense. They included
the idea that prices needed to be pushed up to make recovery possible,
whereas competition constrained recovery by driving prices down. They
held that big firms in industry—those "too big to fail"—were to write
codes for all members of their sector, large and small—which naturally
worked to the advantage of those larger firms. As for consumer choice,
it was deemed inefficient and an inhibitor of recovery. The absurdity
of these principles was overlooked, however, because they were put
forth by great minds. One member of the Brains Trust, Ray Moley,
described the myopic credentialism of his fellow Brains Truster, Felix
Frankfurter, in this way:

> The problems of economic life were matters to be settled in a
> law office, a court room, or around a labor-management bar-
> gaining table. These problems were litigious, controversial,
> not broadly constructive and evolutionary. The government
> was the protagonist. Its agents were its lawyers and commis-
> sioners. The antagonists were big corporate lawyers. In the
> background were misty principals whom Frankfurter never
> really knew at first hand and who were chiefly envisaged
> as concepts in legalistic fencing. Those background figures
> were owners of the corporations, managers, workers and
> consumers.[3]

One family that was targeted by NRA bureaucrats was the Schechters, who were wholesale chicken butchers in Brooklyn. The NRA
code that aimed to regulate what they did was called The Code of Fair
Competition for the Live Poultry Industry of the Metropolitan Area
in and about the City of New York. And according to this code, the
Schechters did all the wrong things. They paid their butchers too little.
They charged prices that were too low. They allowed their customers
to pick their own chickens. Worst of all, they sold a sick chicken. As a
result of these supposed crimes, they were prosecuted.

The prosecution would have been comic if it were not business
tragedy. Imagine the court room scene: On one side stands Walter

Lyman Rice, a graduate of Harvard Law School, representing the government. On the other stands a small man in the poultry trade, Louis Spatz, who is afraid of going to jail. Spatz tries to defend his actions. But he barely speaks English, and the prosecutor bullies him. Nevertheless, Spatz is now and then able to articulate, in his simple and common-sense way, how business really works.

> *Prosecution:* But you do not claim to be an expert?
> *Spatz:* No.
> *Prosecution:* On the competitive practices in the live poultry industry?
> *Spatz:* I would want to get paid, if I was an expert.
> *Prosecution:* You are not an expert!
> *Spatz:* I am experienced, but not an expert....
> *Prosecution:* You have not studied agricultural economics?
> *Spatz:* No, sir.
> *Prosecution:* Or any sort of economics?
> *Spatz:* No, sir.
> *Prosecution:* What is your education?
> *Spatz:* None; very little.
> *Prosecution:* None at all?
> *Spatz:* Very little.

Then at one point this everyman sort of pulls himself together.

> *Prosecution:* And you would not endeavor to explain economic consequences of competitive practices?
> *Spatz:* In my business I am the best economist.
> *Prosecution:* What is that?
> *Spatz:* In my business I am the best economizer.
> *Prosecution:* You are the best economizer?
> *Spatz:* Yes, without figuring.
> *Prosecution:* I wish to have that word spelled in the minutes, just as he stated it.
> *Spatz:* I do not know how to spell.[4]

This dialogue matters because little businesses like Schechter Poultry are the natural drivers of recovery, and during the Great Depression they weren't allowed to do that driving. They weren't allowed to compete and accumulate wealth—or, in terms of *Monopoly*, to place a house or hotel on their property. Instead, they were sidelined. The Schechter brothers ultimately won their case in the Supreme Court in 1935. But the cost of the lawsuits combined with the Depression did not go away.

Regarding monetary policy, it is clear that there wasn't enough money in the early 1930s. So Roosevelt was not wrong in trying to reflate. But though his general idea was right, the discretionary aspect of his policy was terrifying. As Henry Morgenthau reports in his diaries, prices were set by the president personally. FDR took the U.S. off the gold standard in April 1933, and by summer he was setting the gold price every morning from his bed. Morgenthau reports that at one point the president ordered the gold price up 21 cents. Why 21, Morgenthau asked. Roosevelt replied, because it's 3 x 7, and three is a lucky number. "If anybody ever knew how we really set the gold price…" wrote Morgenthau in his diary, "they would be frightened."[5]

Discretionary policies aimed at cleaning up Wall Street were destructive as well. The New Dealers attacked the wealthy as "money changers" and "Princes of Property." In his second inaugural address, delivered in 1937 after his reelection, Roosevelt described government as an instrument of "unimagined power" that should be used to "fashion a higher order of things." This caused business to freeze in its tracks. Companies went on what Roosevelt himself resentfully termed a "capital strike."

These capital strikers mattered because they were even more important to recovery than the Schechters. Consider the case of Alfred Lee Loomis, who had the kind of mind that could contribute significantly to Gross Domestic Product and job creation. During the First World War, he had improved the design of firearms for the U.S. Army. In the 1920s, he became wealthy through his work in investment banking. He moved in a crowd that was developing a new form of utility company that might finally be able to marshal the capital to bring electricity to the American South. But when Loomis saw that the Roosevelt administration was hauling utilities executives down to Washington for hearings, he shut down his business, retreated to his Tudor house, and ran a kind of private think tank for his own benefit.

We have heard a lot about a labor surfeit in the 1930s. Here is a heresy: What if there was a shortage of talent brought on by declarations of class warfare?

Another challenge to the Depression economy was tax increases. While these increases didn't achieve the social equality at which they aimed, they did significant damage by confiscating too much individual and corporate property. As a result, many individuals and businesses simply reduced or halted production—especially as the New Deal wore on. In the late 1930s, banker Leonard Ayres of the Cleveland Trust Company said in the *New York Times*: "For nearly a decade now the great majority of corporations have been losing money instead of making it."[6]

As for big labor, the Wagner Act of 1935 proved to be quite destructive. It brought on drastic changes at factories, including the closed shop—the exclusion of nonunion members. Another innovation it helped bring about was the sit-down strike, which threatened the basic property right of factory owners to close their doors. Most importantly, it gave unions the power to demand higher wages—and they did. A wage chart for the twentieth century shows that real wages in the 1930s were higher than the trend for the rest of the century. This seems perverse, considering the economic conditions at the time. The result was high paying jobs for a few and high unemployment for everyone else. The reality of overpriced labor can be seen in several stock phrases coming out of the Great Depression—"Nice work if you can get it," for example, was the refrain of a Gershwin song performed by Fred Astaire in *The Damsel in Distress*, a film released in 1937 at the zenith of union power.

To return to the *Monopoly* board metaphor, the problem in the 1930s was not that there was no bank. It was that there was too much bank—in the form of the federal government. The government took an arbitrary approach to the money supply and made itself the most powerful player. It shoved everyone else aside so that it could monopolize the board. Benjamin Anderson, a Chase economist at the time, summed it up in a book about the period: "Preceding chapters have explained the Great Depression of 1930 to 1939 as due to the efforts of the governments and very especially the government of the United States to play god."[7]

Relevance for Today

It is not hard to see some of today's troubles as a repeat of the errors of the 1930s. There is arrogance up top. The federal government is dilettantish with money and exhibits disregard and even hostility to all other players. It is only as a result of this that economic recovery seems out of reach.

The key to recovery, now as in the 1930s, is to be found in property rights. These rights suffer under our current politics in several ways. The mortgage crisis, for example, arose out of a long-standing erosion of the property rights concept—first on the part of Fannie Mae and Freddie Mac, but also on that of the Federal Reserve. Broadening FDR's entitlement theories, Congress taught the country that home ownership was a "right." This fostered a misunderstanding of what property is. The owners didn't realize what ownership entailed—that is, they didn't grasp that they were obligated to deliver on the terms of the contract of their mortgage. In the bipartisan enthusiasm for making everyone an owner, our government debased the concept of home ownership.

Property rights are endangered as well by the ongoing assault on contracts generally. A perfect example of this was the treatment of Chrysler bonds during the company's bankruptcy, where senior secured creditors were ignored, notwithstanding the status of their bonds under bankruptcy law. The current administration made a political decision to subordinate those contracts to union demands. That sent a dangerous signal for the future that U.S. bonds are not trustworthy.

Three other threats to property loom. One is tax increases, such as the coming expiration of the Bush tax cuts. More taxes mean less private property. A second threat is in the area of infrastructure. Stimulus plans tend to emphasize infrastructure—especially roads and railroads. And after the Supreme Court's *Kelo* decision of 2005, the federal government will have enormous license to use eminent domain to claim private property for these purposes. Third and finally, there is the worst kind of confiscation of private property: inflation, which excessive government spending necessarily encourages. Many of us sense that inflation is closer than the country thinks.

If the experience of the Great Depression teaches anything, it is that property rights must be firmly established or else we will not have the kind of economic activity that leads to strong recovery. The *Monopoly* board game reminds us that economic growth isn't mysterious and inscrutable. Economic growth depends on the impulse of the small businessman and entrepreneur to get back in the game. In order for this to happen, we don't need a perfect government. All we need is one that is "not too bad," whose rules are not constantly changing and snuffing out the willingness of these players to take risks. We need a government under which the money supply doesn't change unpredictably, there are not too many "Go to Jail" cards, and the top hats are confident in the possibility of seeing significant returns on investment.

Recovery won't happen from the top. But when those at the top step back and create the proper conditions, it will happen down there on the board—one house at a time.

Notes

1. "New Games for Parlor," *New York Times*, November 24, 1935.
2. Quoted in Ben Yagoda, *Will Rogers: A Biography* (New York: Knopf, 1993), 302.
3. Raymond Moley, *27 Masters of Politics* (New York: Funk & Wagnall's Co., 1949), 152.
4. *Schechter Poultry Corp.* v. *United States.*
5. John Morton Blum, ed., *From the Morgenthau Diaries* (Boston: Houghton Mifflin, 1959–1967).
6. "Wages and Profits," *New York Times*, December 24, 1938.
7. Benjamin McAlester Anderson, *Economics and the Public Welfare: A Financial and Economic History of the United States, 1914–1946* (New York: Van Nostrand, 1949), 495.

LARRY SCHWEIKART

The Economic and Political Legacy
of the New Deal

When Michael Allen and I published *A Patriot's History of the United States* in 2004, we included what I thought was a unique chart. It was a three-page table of selected New Deal programs that showed their intended results and their long-term effects after 50 years. It makes the point, starkly and briefly, that not only did the New Deal fail in most of its immediate goals, but that in the long haul it severely damaged the United States in a number of ways. What the chart did not include was the political legacy of Franklin Roosevelt's programs. Since the publication of *Patriot's History*, yet another legacy has become evident—an educational legacy—and that should be added as well.

In the past few years, the nation has faced the collapse of several major banks and the bankruptcy of its leading automaker. During this time, many of the policies undertaken to restore the system to health were conceived—and some directly carried out—by the chairman of the Federal Reserve System, Ben Bernanke. At this point, only the most diehard Democrat would argue that any of these policies have worked. The "Troubled Asset Relief Program," a sort of modern-day Reconstruction Finance Administration, purchased "troubled assets" (also called "toxic assets") from banks to encourage financial institutions to

61

resume lending, which it has not. A few months later, Congress passed the controversial "stimulus" spending package, supposedly packed with "shovel-ready jobs," that has since seen unemployment go from 4.6% in January 2007 to over 10% today. (And some analysts think that rate fails to capture the true unemployment rate, which they argue is closer to 16% when including those who have quit looking for work.) And General Motors? The government bailout of the auto giant was supposed to save jobs—whereupon GM promptly slashed 13,000 from its payroll. Of the 111,000 hourly workers General Motors employed under President George W. Bush, today it has only 48,000.[1]

Why is it so ironic that Bernanke—*Time* magazine's Man of the Year in 2009—would have had a voice, and often a direct hand, in so much of this? It is because Bernanke's claim to fame as a scholar was his work on the Great Depression, and it should be thought if anyone would have "learned the lessons" of the Depression, it would have been him.[2] Bernanke's prominent role in trying to prevent a deflation by turning the printing presses to what my old rock-and-roll bandmates would call "stomp" indicates that our fiscal and monetary policies are still very much influenced by the events of 80 years ago. The fear of reliving that experience often leads otherwise level-headed people such as George W. Bush to insist that he had to abandon free market principles in order to save the free market system.[3] Was this not, in many ways, the same argument made by Franklin Roosevelt in 1933?

We continue to pay a steep price for failing to understand the causes and the proper responses to the Great Depression. Certainly what understanding we do have has not been aided by mainstream historians, who have done their best to blame business for the collapse and praise government for saving the Republic. For example, in *The Enduring Vision*, Paul Boyer and his colleagues insist that the "income tax cuts proposed by Treasury Secretary Andrew Mellon had increased the volume of money available for speculation," while Jeanne Boydston, et al., chimed in: "Like the banks, the investment industry was free from regulation and given to misrepresentation, manipulation of stock prices, and inside deals."[4] Irwin Unger wrote in *These United States* that "Americans have often blamed the stock market collapse for their plight in the 1930s. The blame is not entirely misplaced....

the 1920s had been a time of economic growth, but that economic growth depended on an unstable balance of factors.... With 50 percent of the nation's income going to only 20 percent of its families, the market...was limited."[5]

Indeed, almost all textbooks accept the story line that the tax cuts of the 1920s caused a speculative boom in the stock market, which then helped bring on the Great Depression. Most historians accept these premises—and yet few economists do. One of the few economists who still clings to the tax cuts/big business explanation is Christina Romer, who advises President Barack Obama today, but even she temporizes her claims.[6] Otherwise, the last two "big name" economists to hold this view were John Maynard Keynes (*General Theory of Employment, Interest and Money*, 1936) and John Kenneth Galbraith (*The Great Crash, 1929* [1955]), from whom, apparently, most historians took their views. According to this interpretation, the "big banks" and their brokerage affiliates siphoned money out of depositors accounts to "play the market," weakening the banks and driving up stock prices. Then, for reasons never quite explained by the historians, the "bubble burst" (or words to that effect) and the Crash triggered a banking panic. This narrative blames Republican President Herbert Hoover for not doing enough—despite the fact that under his administration the Reconstruction Finance Corporation was established—and causing more banking uncertainty and weakness. At any rate, the tale ends when the shining knight, Franklin D. Roosevelt rides in on his limousine, brandishing his cigarette holder, to "save the system" by punishing business, raising taxes, and restoring the banks. As I said in my recent book, *48 Liberal Lies About American History*, "since virtually all major college textbooks adopt some version of this, I'll spare [you] a five-page footnote."[7]

When one gets into the details, however, most of this narrative falls apart. Sure the stock market boomed, but studies have shown that stockholders were generally well-informed that a "bubble" was either nonexistent or minimal in that the stock values correlated closely with the real values of the companies, and that investments were held by a wide cross section of Americans.[8] Even Eugene White, who argued for the presence of a bubble, dismissed any notion that it might have constituted a major source of instability.[9] But White did insist that the presence of "securities affiliates" (i.e., brokerage houses) attached to banks did not weaken them, but in fact made them more stable with better diversification.[10] Nor has there been conclusive evidence that "insiders" knew the crash was coming, but "average people" did not.[11] Where most economists do agree is with Milton Friedman and Anna Schwartz that the Fed failed to inject enough liquidity into the system to prevent the one-third drop in the money supply from 1929 to 1932—but that had been going on for most of the decade, as the Fed had consistently failed to keep the money supply up with production.[12]

So the first legacy of the Great Depression is neither economic nor political, but educational, namely that for almost 70 years, economists have been rejecting the "stock market/big business" causation of the Great Depression, while historians unanimously accept it. Until recently, economists downplayed the impact of the Smoot-Hawley Tariff as the key government action that was most responsible for the economic downturn. Jude Wanniski, a nonacademic economist, started the discussion in 1978 with his book *The Way the World Works*, arguing from correlation that the march of the tariff through the Congress matched rises and falls in the stock market, and since Smoot-Hawley portended to be (at the time) the single largest tax hike in history, it was only reasonable to assume that it played a role in the Great Crash. Wanniski argued that the key committee vote triggered the final collapse of stock prices as manufacturers immediately attempted to get liquidity by selling their own assets and to anticipate higher prices for their products, thus, lower sales and profits.[13]

Because Wanniski wasn't an academic, there was a certain snobbish reluctance on the part of scholars to fully embrace his views, but slowly the studies began to appear showing that Smoot-Hawley had produced instant investment uncertainty and had shocked prices. The market plunged with each new hurdle in Congress that the tariff crossed.[14] In fact, the more that people studied the Smoot-Hawley Tariff, the worse it looked, with Doug Irwin concluding that, when taken in the context of the shrinking money supply, the real-value impact of the Tariff on the U.S. economy was close to 5 percent of GNP. To put it in perspective, that meant that the Smoot-Hawley Tariff as an economic event was 1.5 times greater than the economic impact of the 9/11 attacks or the Arab Oil Crisis in 1973, and ten times greater than Hurricane Katrina.[15] Certainly when combining the pernicious effects of government policies—whether Smoot-Hawley or Hoover's RFC, which, by publishing the names of troubled banks in papers, often weakened them further and subjected them to runs—there isn't much room to blame the private sector for the Great Depression.

Once Franklin Roosevelt entered the picture, however, any hope of a recovery vanished. FDR and John F. Kennedy have gotten by far the best "press" of any presidents in U.S. history textbooks, mostly due to clever selection of facts by historians and to the tendency of liberals to judge people by their intentions, not their results. Roosevelt's single success story is the one almost universally overlooked by historians in lieu of a program that was not particularly effective, namely, he took the nation off the gold standard in 1933 and, in the course of the "Bank Holiday," established federal deposit insurance through the Federal Deposit Insurance Corporation, which was made permanent in 1934.[16] Here, even sensible business historians such as Joseph Pusateri gushed "no single legislative step did more to restore, calm, and reduce the likelihood of further panics."[17] Rather, once the United States shut the gold window—one of the few nations left paying gold on paper currency—the runs stopped. Insurance had little to do with it.[18] Quite the contrary, Charles Calomiris has shown that state deposit insurance played a major role in destabilizing banks in states that had mandatory deposit insurance, while branch banking was the most powerful innovation to strengthen banks. Had FDR truly been the trailblazer so many wished to see him as, he would have instituted nationwide branch banking.[19]

Given that the Bank Holiday and the institution of deposit insurance were among the first New Deal programs enacted, theirs is the first legacy we should examine. While banks solidified in the 1930s and the nation saw no new waves of failures, severe weaknesses of the Federal Deposit Insurance Corporation nevertheless existed. These became apparent in the sister program, the Federal Savings and Loan Insurance Corporation (FSLIC), created in 1934 to insure the deposits of savings and loan institutions (S&Ls). Administered by the Federal Home Loan Bank Board, FSLIC operated quietly until the savings and loan crisis of the 1980s. But the crisis itself had been building for years, largely the result of the high inflation of the Jimmy Carter years. As inflation drove up the cost of money, S&Ls had to pay more to attract deposits, but were prohibited by law from doing so. This caused people to withdraw their savings—a process called "disintermediation." In addition, S&L regulation made it impossible for those institutions to offer checking accounts. So S&Ls had no way to generate income, and no way to attract new deposits to offer more mortgages. The government sought to save the thrift industry with the Depository Institutions Deregulation and Monetary Control Act (1980) and the Garn-St. Germain Depository Institutions Act (1982) that freed the S&Ls to pay more for deposits and to offer quasi-checking accounts for the first time.

This introduced the concept of "moral hazard" into the S&Ls (but not the banks, which were not regulated as to their deposit interest). "Moral hazard" is defined as encouraging the very behavior one hopes to prevent. The S&L owners and managers were desperate, and realized the trend lines were against them. They could not remain in "safe" investments with the small percentages of nonmortgage loans they were allowed to make and hope to catch up with the losses on the fixed mortgages. But since the depositors were "covered" by Uncle Sam, the owners and managers could roll the dice and invest in risky ventures, mostly land. When the land market crashed, so did the S&Ls. When the FSLIC was terminated after accumulating losses of $100 billion between 1984 and 1989, as the number of S&Ls dwindled from 6,000 to 2,934, it should have set off alarm bells that perhaps the entire concept of deposit insurance itself was flawed, but except for a few economists, few noticed.[20] It is somewhat ironic, then, that the FDIC, which did not save the banks in 1933, is usually thought to have done so; while the FSLIC, which did contribute directly to the destruction of the thrift industry, often escapes blame—but such is what passes for history writing these days.[21]

Confident the banks were saved, Roosevelt moved on to the labor markets. While Keynes's *General Theory* would not appear for three more years, by 1933 his ideas had permeated much of the political class, including FDR's "Brains Trust." Briefly, Keynes thought that the cause of the Depression had been underconsumption (or, to paraphrase former South Carolina Senator Fritz Hollings, "too much savin' goin' on out dere"), and that the solution lay in a "stimulus package" (sound familiar?) in which the U.S. government would put money into the hands of people whose demand would then spark production. "Demand-side" economics, as it is known, has been a common treatment for recessions ever since, usually involving a small, targeted tax cut that would encourage people to buy an appliance or other mid-sized item. Keynes's strategy called for a widespread spending program by government in labor markets through job creation, and simply put, it amounted to the maxim, "money in, everything else up." Roosevelt's advisors, therefore, embarked on numerous programs designed to put people to work doing anything—the actual product of the labor wasn't as important as the fact that men (mostly) drew a paycheck that they would then spend, generating economic growth.

Responses in the New Deal included the Civilian Conservation Corps, intended to put men to work on reclamation and forestry projects, or, as Roosevelt's supporters said, send "boys into the forests to get us out of the woods."[22] Two larger programs, the Public Works Administration and the Works Progress Administration, pressed people into all sorts of projects, from building airports to painting murals to laying sidewalks to writing slave narratives. Some of their work products were indeed useful—Dayton, Ohio, still has WPA sidewalks downtown, and the Mill Avenue Bridge in Tempe, Arizona, remains a thoroughfare across the Salt River. PWA money also linked Florida's mainland with Key West; built the Lincoln Tunnel; and paid for construction of two Navy carriers, the *Yorktown* and *Enterprise*. So there is no question that some of the work was important, though in a free market economy, one wonders what voters would have thought about being taxed directly for the luxury of hooking up Key West or of throwing up airplane hangars. The value of other work was dubious, at best: Opera houses were built during a decade when average Americans struggled to put together enough money for a movie, and travel guides were written for people who didn't have cars, let alone the money or time for a vacation.

By their nature, however, the programs were intended to be visible, for a job not seen is a vote not won—thus, the bigger the project, the better. And not unlike current politicians, Roosevelt had a mouth that came with two distinct sides, warning that welfare was "a narcotic, a subtle destroyer of the human spirit" even while pretending that make-work did not constitute welfare.[23] Critics had a different view, calling the WPA "We Piddle Around," but while one could question the need for some of the half-million miles of roads, 100,000 bridges, and 200 airfields, the real value of the program was that it permitted the facade of government "make work" to provide dignity to a generation of men still steeped in the work ethic that told them that pure welfare was a con, a trap, and above all, unmanly.

Two movies capture this dynamic in very different ways. *Seabiscuit*, released in 2003, told the story of the undersized Depression-era champion racehorse, with the subtext of the New Deal putting the "little guy" back to work and restoring dignity. Two years later, a much different view of "workfare" was depicted in the film *Cinderella Man*, about boxer Jim Braddock who beat Max Baer for the world heavyweight title in 1935. Struggling to support his family by working part time on the docks—often with a broken hand—Braddock eventually had to go on welfare. However, after his championship match, he marched into the welfare office and paid back every cent (and later served as a First Lieutenant in the Pacific teaching hand-to-hand combat). In one film—*Seabiscuit*—government jobs are portrayed as dignifying, while in the other, any government aid, whether jobs or welfare, constituted an attack on man's independence. Which, would you say, better represents the typical attitude in America today, where middle- and upper-class American families not only accept, but lustfully pursue federal college aid; where Social Security is considered a "right"; and where the attitude toward unemployment checks is "I've earned it"?

It is fair to say, then, that one of the chief economic legacies of the New Deal involved a complete makeover of the concept of dignity as derived from labor. Gone was the notion that for labor to be dignified, it had to benefit others; in its place was a Marxian perversion of work that instilled a value on any labor, useful or otherwise. If, after all, the goal was to get a paycheck in a person's pocket, then it stood to reason that the government would end up, as it did, paying for traveling circuses.[24] The very fact that so many men fooled themselves into thinking that simply drawing a paycheck imbued them with intrinsic worth constituted a regime change of the highest order, and has subsequently infected much of the private sector. While there is an argument that in the 1950s and 1960s many Americans lived for their jobs, and believed (at their own peril, we now know) that corporations were "families" who would take care of them no matter what, the modern generations have swung radically the other direction, viewing work as substantially what one does so that one can play. A key objective of restoring the world to a pre-New Deal mentality must therefore be a reelevation of the place of work in society, not as the all-encompassing end of one's life, but as dignified in and of itself when...and only when...it produces value for others. Put another way, the separation of serving one's fellow man as a precondition of dignified labor was one of the New Deal's most enduring, and destructive, legacies.

Another economic legacy—one with remarkable overtones for recent months—involved the attempt by Roosevelt to control prices. Low farm prices had plagued the agricultural sector for a decade, the result of too many farmers (not just in America, but around the world). Agricultural productivity increases demanded that many farmers find other employment, but instead they went hat in hand to the government, resulting in a host of programs designed to ensure a fixed income. None of these succeeded. Roosevelt's "Brains Trust" had a different approach: They would try to force a cut in production by subsidizing farmers who took some of their land out of cultivation. The government would make up the difference. Farmers dutifully plowed up 10 million acres of cotton, and Midwestern hog growers eliminated nine million pounds of pork as cities struggled to fill soup kitchens with food. Yet instead of curtailing production, farmers overplanted on existing lands and took the checks, too. Worse, the entire premise is goofy: What would Hillsdale's trustees think about paying professors not to teach so that the "value" of the few classes they do teach goes up? Or how about rewarding students who do not study, do not turn in papers, and do not take exams with higher grades? It was a preposterously flawed theory, but farm subsidies stuck with us en masse until the Republicans captured Congress in 1994 and did away with many of them. But even today, some remain.

There are many, many more economic legacies of the New Deal I could discuss, including the notion that government should have greater control and oversight over the banking system (and in light of Barney Frank and Christopher Dodd's recent incompetence in that arena, I would say the case against that is obvious), or the National Recovery Administration, which both Burton Folsom and Amity Shlaes, in their books, have brutally exposed.[25] But one area that has escaped widespread analysis in most U.S. history books, the impact of the minimum wage law on labor markets, is an aspect of the New Deal that speaks directly to what I consider to be the long-term failure of Roosevelt's programs to generate any significant reduction in the unemployment rates. For example, Eric Foner's *Give Me Liberty* doesn't mention any connection between higher (mandatory) wages and continued unemployment; nor do James Roark, et al. in *American Promise*; nor do Jeanne Boydston, et al., in *Making a Nation*.[26]

One reason virtually no textbooks connect the National Industrial Recovery Administration (NIRA) or the subsequent Fair Labor Standards Act (i.e., the minimum wage law) to the prolonged depression in the labor market is the date. In part, historians accepted the 1938 passage of the law itself as the starting point for minimum wages, when in fact the inability of industry to respond to the real value of labor was contained in the minimum wage provisions of the NIRA, signed into law in June 1933 and effectively up and running by early 1934. Economist Stephen DeCanio, looking at man-hours worked rather than number of workers employed—because the hours worked tended to vary a great deal, isolated the share of business expectations related to man-hours and to future hiring (versus, say, raw materials). He found that "expectations deteriorated almost monotonically after the stock market crash until...late 1932...then rapidly recovered." But the man-hours index in manufacturing "fell to its lowest level in late 1932, and although it recovered somewhat," it never attained more than about two-thirds of its pre-Crash levels.[27] More important, until mid-1933, most of the decline in unemployment was related to corollary declines in business expectations—

a natural conclusion—but that afterward another factor was at work, the increased real wage level. He attributed that to an "inward shift in the demand for labor in manufacturing [caused by] the NIRA-induced increase in industrial prices."[28] Put another way, after the NIRA put in place minimum wages (long before the "minimum wage law"), accounting for an increase of roughly 25 percent in real wages —at a time when wages should have been falling, to encourage new hires—it was a certainty that those workers who remained on the job would work less, and that no new hiring would occur. Thus, when the "official" minimum wage act went into effect five years later, its impact was already being felt in the labor markets. Even Ben Bernanke agreed, writing that the NIRA also "slowed the recovery by reducing the speed with which wages and prices adjusted."[29]

So, one might ask, what were the Democrats thinking? Harry Hopkins summed it up nicely: "We've got to get everything we want—a works program, social security, wages and hours, everything—now or never."[30] And this is where the political legacy comes in: Every policy FDR put into place served two purposes. First, he intended it to bring about a recovery, and genuinely believed his actions would have a positive effect. So when he said, in 1935, "We are on our way back…we planned it that way," he was stating what he thought to be true.[31] However, each New Deal program contained a second, political, component, which was to place the Democratic Party in a permanent position of dominance in the American political system. Folsom has detailed the extensive specificity with which New Deal aid went to districts in which Democrat candidates needed votes. Beyond that, however, Roosevelt took Reconstruction-era antagonisms and repackaged them with class envy on a massive new scale, raging against the "plutocrats." Harold Ickes claimed "sixty families" sought to control the nation and that the struggle against them must be "fought through to a finish."[32] In criticisms of corporate executives that predated Barack Obama, Assistant Attorney General Robert Jackson singled out leading businessmen and complained about their high salaries.[33] Of course, once business truly came into the gun sights of government, money followed, as companies sought to bribe or appease their potential attackers, causing an influx of corporate lobby-

ing money into government on a scale never before seen. Taxes—and
audits—suddenly became political weapons in the president's arsenal,
and Roosevelt wielded both liberally. When Rexford Tugwell complained to FDR that some of the Social Security taxes were disproportionately hard on the poor, Roosevelt said "those taxes were never
…economics. They are politics all the way."[34]

Bribes of another sort, namely policies specifically directed at
securing a monopoly position for labor unions through the National
Labor Relations Act, succeeded beyond Roosevelt's wildest dreams.
Well into the twenty-first century, unions (particularly the heavy
industrial unions) have supported the Democratic Party almost unanimously. Ronald Reagan achieved a remarkable victory when he won
the vote of the Teamsters Union in the 1980s. By building in a bias
against businesses, the Wagner Act (as the NLRA was called) threw
government's weight against any business that did not bargain "in
good faith," meaning against any business that wasn't negotiating in
a manner that pleased the government.

Not only did Roosevelt use direct bribes in the form of federal
"aid" to districts that needed to elect Democrats, and not only did he
revise federal laws to disproportionately benefit labor unions, but he
sought to move an entire generation of people, the elderly, onto Democrat voting rolls through the Social Security Act, which is clearly one
of the most enduring New Deal legacies. By 2001, nearly one-third of
all retirees received 90 percent of their income or more from Social
Security, and almost two-thirds depended on the program for half of
their retirement income.[35] When the program started, as many as 14
employees paid into the so-called "Social Security Trust Fund" (which
has long since been abandoned as a genuine separate fund and blended
in with general revenues) to every retiree taking out. By 2009, the ratio
had changed to about three paying in for every one taking out; and
within a few years, the number will be one paying in for every three
taking out. Most estimates have Social Security turning into the red
(more money going out than coming in) within a decade—but if the
economic downturn pushes more people into early retirement, that
schedule could be accelerated. At any rate, even optimistic projections
have the entire "Trust Fund" depleted by about 2040.

While there seems little doubt that Roosevelt wanted to ensure a growing voting block of "oldsters," even he did not anticipate that Social Security would become the sole means of support for so many, and in his 1935 message to Congress, he insisted that it should only be supplemental, and that the majority of a person's retirement funding should come from private savings. As one of his four pieces of legislation related to "economic security," FDR proposed "voluntary contributory annuities by which individual initiative can increase amounts received in old age."[36] Then Roosevelt made a statement that might astonish modern-day liberals, who become apoplectic when someone mentions fixing Social Security: "It is proposed that the Federal Government assume one-half of the cost of the old-age pension plan, which ought ultimately to be *supplanted* by self-supporting annuity plans [emphasis mine]," or, one could say, by a private system.[37] Even Roosevelt must have known that the system would soon be subjected to ridiculous mismatches, such as Ida May Fuller, who paid into the Social Security system for only three years before retiring, contributing a net of $24.75, then, upon retirement, receiving a monthly check of $22.54...for her lifetime! Fuller received some $23,000 from the Social Security system.[38]

Another component of the original Social Security Act was funds to be given to the states to help destitute elderly and children (the term at the time was "outdoor" relief as opposed to "indoor" relief), and was almost always restricted to destitute widows.[39] The words "families with" were added to the name in 1960 out of a concern that the rules would discourage marriage, which, of course, they did. Charles Murray's *Losing Ground* showed that the key change occurred under the Great Society—Lyndon Johnson's attempt at a "New Deal."[40] Murray found that word changes in AFDC made it advantageous for unmarried people to live together; for married people to get divorced; and, above all, for women to live alone rather than with a man working a minimum wage job. When combined with the concentration of African-Americans in inner cities (as opposed to poorer whites, who were rural), welfare workers disproportionately enlisted blacks onto welfare rolls. Thus, illegitimacy among blacks actually rose slower than among whites from 1950 to 1975, but because black illegitimacy was much higher to start, the changes in AFDC caused an epidemic of illegitimacy among blacks. By 1994, when the Republicans undertook reform of the welfare system for the first time, the illegitimacy rate topped 70 percent.[41] When Johnson first decided to "fix" poverty in the early 1960s, the rate was only 22 percent! Moreover, by 2002, the U.S. percentage of new mothers who were unwed neared 40 percent.

While all of this is not to be laid at the feet of the AFDC program, or, indirectly, the New Deal, much of it is. And one could reasonably argue that even for that percentage not given direct financial incentives, the moral barriers against unwed motherhood were nearly destroyed by the liberal programs (with a healthy dose of the media thrown in). Or, whatever changes in family dynamics the policies themselves did not cause, the cultural shifts they provoked accounted for the rest. When one then adds to the mix the crime and teen unemployment associated with the effects of illegitimacy, then stirs in the collapse of many (most?) inner-city public school systems, the New Deal legacy stands out as a phenomenally destructive gift to many generations of Americans in this arena alone.

There is no doubt FDR used the tax system and justice department to attack and harass his enemies, including Samuel Insull, Charles Mitchell, Huey Long, as well as many lesser-known individuals Folsom details in *New Deal or Raw Deal?* The larger questions of whether he employed the New Deal as a means to secure permanent Democratic majorities is less clear. Certainly if he was trying to do so, aligning labor and the elderly with the Party through massive buyoffs would have been the proper strategy. Contrary to the views of some, I do not think he implemented the "welfare state" with the intention of creating a permanent dependent class: even for Roosevelt, that would have been a view out of step with his times, in which work still held dignity, and in which the government was to be the last, not first, resort.

As for using the political system against one's enemies, this was nothing new either. Martin Van Buren and Andrew Jackson had designed the modern-day Democratic Party to use the "Spoils System" and patronage to ensure loyalty over personal ideology.[42] This, the first widespread use of political organization as a means to perpetuate power, naturally lacked polish. It was clumsy and above all, small potatoes compared to the later efforts of the Radical Republicans or the New Dealers, but it was an effort just the same. The Jacksonians redistributed money from the Bank of the United States to their political pals, hired editors and started their own newspapers, and changed the entire election structure permanently, tying votes to government largesse. Thirty years later, the Radical Republicans in Congress, building on the Jacksonian model, wielded the powers of the bureaucracy even more ruthlessly. They sought to remove or gag military officials who did not accept their approach to Reconstruction, forced the installation of puppets in important parts of the federal bureaucracy, and created the prototype New Deal program in the Freedmen's Bureau. Historian Paul Johnson described the Freedmen's Bureau as "America's first taste of the welfare state, even before it was established by its European progenitor, Bismarck's Germany."[43] By attempting to lure blacks onto government aid and assistance, and by slipping federal money in to build schools, the Freedmen's Bureau lived down to Johnson's description.

There is little doubt that the Radicals—having seen the Democrats as responsible for both slavery and the war—sought to permanently destroy the Democratic Party. But the very patronage system that Van Buren created ensured that such a goal was difficult to obtain, for all anyone needed to get elected was the reasonable likelihood that he could reward you with a job once in office. Thus, each election, even under the Radicals, became a contest of government giveaways, flooding the machinery of government with so many job applicants that it took months for presidents to sign the paperwork (at a time when the government remained a tiny fraction of what it is today). Worse, the system arguably got President James Garfield killed, igniting a wave of reform, culminating with the Pendleton Civil Service Act (1883), which established civil service exams and made many government jobs "nonpolitical," meaning one could only be removed for malfeasance or incompetence. (As hard as it may be to imagine, the architects of the act did expect that some government employees would have to be fired!)

On the surface, the Pendleton Act killed the Van Buren patronage system, but in reality, it did just the opposite: Since individual politicians could no longer promise a handful of customs commissioners' jobs in order to get a sufficient number of votes, they had to widen the net. Consequently, Pendleton shifted the "spoils system" from a relatively personal and low-level exercise in rewarding cronies to a much more destructive "shotgun" approach of promising broad-based benefits to vast "special-interest" groups. One now had to go to the Grand Army of the Republic, or the "sugar trust," or the American Federation of Labor instead of merely meeting in a "smoke-filled room" with a handful of bosses who would get political plum jobs. Whereas American government grew steadily, but slowly, from 1824 to 1860, after Pendleton it expanded geometrically with every election.

Roosevelt, then, had all the political inclinations of the early Jacksonians and the Radical Republicans, but possessed of political power they only dreamed of. Studies of his largesse reveal that supporters and their regions gained disproportionately from New Deal funding—a tactic copied by the Obama administration, which directed the larger share of so-called "stimulus money" to Democrat districts.[44] As Raymond Moley promised, "Patronage would be used, if not as a club, then as a steel-pointed pic."[45] As Folsom noted, based on the polling of the Deputy Director of the Democratic National Committee Emil Hurja and James Farley, the Postmaster General and a Roosevelt confidant, the most important question they could ask was, "What swing states (or congressional districts) would benefit from special injections of federal dollars?"[46] It was a question the Jacksonians could not have asked, and a question the Radicals would have asked and answered—but lacked the means to address. The economic and political legacy of Franklin Roosevelt's New Deal, therefore, is that not only did he ask the question of how taxpayer money could be used to keep the Democrats in power, and not only did he answer it ("it can, and it should"), but for the first time a president had it in his power to make it a reality. Perhaps the most astounding thing about the New Deal—and Roosevelt's intentions—is that in spite of all that power, the Democrats did lose elections, and at least some minor elements of his scheme have been rolled back or attenuated, although the current administration seems bent on not only reliving the New Deal, but surpassing it.

Notes

1. Incredibly, the headline at one news source was "GM's Announcement of
   no More Layoffs is Good News After Years of Hemorrhaging Jobs," http://
   www.mlive.com/michigan-job-search/index.ssf/2009/12/gms_announcement_
   of_no_more_is_good_news.html.
2. See, for example, Ben Bernanke, *Essays on the Great Depression* (Princeton, NJ:
   Princeton University Press, 2005); "Nonmonetary Effects of the Financial Crisis
   in the Propagation of the Great Depression," *American Economic Review* 73(3):
   257–76.
3. "Bush on the Economy," http://www.breitbart.tv/?p=242763.
4. Paul S. Boyer, et al., *The Enduring Vision: A History of the American People*, 5th ed.,
   Volume 2: From 1865 (New York: Houghton Mifflin, 2004), 745; Jeanne Boydston,
   et al., *Making a Nation: The United States and Its People*, combined vol. (Upper Saddle
   River, NJ: Pearson, 2004), 570.
5. Irwin Unger, *These United States: Questions of Our Past*, concise ed., combined vol.,
   3rd ed. (Upper Saddle River, NJ: Pearson, 2007), 591.
6. Christina D. Romer, "The Great Crash and the Onset of the Great Depression,"
   Quarterly Journal of Economics 105 (August 1990): 597–624.
7. Larry Schweikart, *48 Liberal Lies About American History (That You Probably Learned
   in School)* (New York: Sentinel, 2009), 222.
8. I have produced an exceptionally long list of sources in endnote 2 in the
   chapter on this in *48 Liberal Lies*, but among just a few of the sources are Gary
   Santoni and Gerald Dwyer, "Bubbles vs. Fundamentals: New Evidence from
   the Great Bull Markets," in Eugene White, *Crises and Panics: The Lessons of History*
   (Homewood, IL: Dow Jones/Irwin, 1990); Peter Rappoport and Eugene White,
   "Was There a Bubble in the 1929 Stock Market?" *Journal of Economic History* 53
   (September 1993): 549–74; R. Glen Donaldson and Mark Kamstra, "A New
   Dividend Forecasting Procedure That Rejects Bubbles in Asset Prices: The Case
   of 1929's Stock Crash," *Review of Financial Studies* 9 (Summer 1996): 333–83;
   and Gene Smiley, *The American Economy in the Twentieth Century* (Cincinnati, OH:
   South-Western Publishing, 1994), chapter 6.
9. Frederic S. Mishkin and Eugene N. White, "U.S. Stock Market Crashes and Their
   Aftermath: Implications for Monetary Policy," in William C. Hunter, George G.
   Kaufman, and Michael Pomerleano, *Asset Price Bubbles: The Implications for Monetary,
   Regulatory, and International Policies* (Cambridge, MA: MIT Press, 2003), 53–79.
10. Eugene N. White, "A Reinterpretation of the Banking Crisis of 1930," *Journal
    of Economic History* 44 (March 1984): 119–38, and his *Regulation and Reform of the
    American Banking System, 1900–29* (Princeton, NJ: Princeton University Press, 1983).
    White found that securities affiliates diversified risk, and that the bank failures of
    the 1920s were not particularly different from previous bank failures.
11. White, "Anticipating the Stock Market Crash of 1929: The View from the Floor
    of the Stock Exchange," NBER Working Papers 12661, National Bureau of

Economic Research, 2006; Edwin J. Perkins, *Wall Street to Main Street: Charles Merrill and Middle-Class Investors* (Cambridge: Cambridge University Press, 2006); Gene Smiley, *Rethinking the Great Depression* (Chicago: Ivan R. Dee, 2002), from uncorrected advance proof, 10–11.

12. Milton Friedman and Anna J. Schwartz, *A Monetary History of the United States, 1867–1960* (Princeton, NJ: Princeton University Press, 1963).

13. Jude Wanniski, *The Way the World Works: How Economies Fail—And Succeed* (New York: Basic Books, 1978).

14. Robert B. Archibald and David H. Feldman, "Investment During the Great Depression: Uncertainty and the Role of the Smoot-Hawley Tariff," *Southern Economic Review* 64 (1998): 857–79; Douglas Irwin, "The Smoot-Hawley Tariff: A Quantitative Assessment," *Review of Economics and Statistics* 80 (May 1998): 326–34; and his "Changes in U.S. Tariffs: The Role of Import Prices and Commercial Policies," *American Economic Review* 88 (September 1998): 1015–26.

15. Doug Irwin, "From Smoot-Hawley to Reciprocal Trade Agreements: Changing the Course of U.S. Trade Policy in the 1930s," in Michael Bordo, et al., *The Defining Moment: The Great Depression and the American Economy in the Twentieth Century* (Chicago: University of Chicago Press, 1998), 325–52; Mario J. Crucini and James Kahn, "Tariffs and Aggregate Economic Activity: Lessons from the Great Depression," *Journal of Monetary Economics* 38, (1996) 427–67; and Crucini's "Sources of Variation in Real Tariff Rates: The United States, 1900–1940," *American Economic Review* 84 (June 1994): 732–43.

16. Larry Schweikart and Lynne Pierson Doti, *American Entrepreneur* (New York: Amacom, 2009), 307–8.

17. C. Joseph Pusateri, *A History of American Business*, 2nd ed. (Arlington Heights, IL: Harlan-Davidson, 1988), 288.

18. Charles Calomiris and Gary Gorton, "The Origins of Banking Panics: Models, Facts, and Bank Regulation," in R. Glenn Hubbard, ed., *Financial Markets and Financial Crises* (Chicago: University of Chicago Press, 1991); Douglas Diamond and Philip Dybvig, "Bank Runs, Deposit Insurance, and Liquidity," *Journal of Political Economy* 91 (June 1983): 401–18.

19. Charles Calomiris, "Is Deposit Insurance Necessary? A Historical Perspective," *Journal of Economic History* 50 (June 1990): 283–96, and his "Deposit Insurance: Lessons from the Record," *Economic Perspectives* 13 (May/June 1989): 10–30.

20. George Bentson and George Kaufman, "Understanding the Savings and Loan Debate," *The Public Interest*, no. 99 (Spring 1990): 79–95; Edward Kane, "FIRREA: Financial Malpractice," *Durrell Journal of Money and Banking* 2 (May 1990): 2–10; Gerald P. O'Driscoll, "Bank Failures: The Deposit Insurance Connection," *Contemporary Policy Issues* 6 (April 1988): 1–12; George Bentson, "Federal Regulation of Banking Analysis and Policy Recommendations," *Journal of Bank Research* 13 (Spring 1983): 93–112; Douglas Diamond and Philip Dybvig, "Bank Runs, Deposit Insurance and Liquidity," *Journal of Political Economy* 91 (June 1983): 401–48.

21. Larry Schweikart, *The Entrepreneurial Adventure: A History of Business in the United States* (Ft. Worth, TX: Harcourt, 2000), 442–44.

22. Larry Schweikart and Michael Allen, *A Patriot's History of the United States from Columbus's Great Discovery to the War on Terror* (New York: Sentinel, 2006), 564.

23. Samuel Rosenman, ed., *The Public Papers and Addresses of Franklin D. Roosevelt* (New York: Random House, 1938–50), 5:19–21.

24. Willson Whitman, *Bread and Circuses: A Study of Federal Theater* (New York: Oxford, 1937); Grant Code, "Dance Theater of the WPA: A Record of National Accomplishment," *Dance Observer* (November 1939): 280–81, 290; "Footlights, Federal Style," *Harper's* 123 (1936): 626; Mabel Ulrich, "Salvaging Culture for the WPA," *Harper's* 78 (1939); "Work of the Federal Writers' Project of the WPA," *Publisher's Weekly* 135 (1939): 1130–35; *Time* 31 (January 3, 1938): 55–56; Robert Binkley, "The Cultural Program of the W.P.A.," *Harvard Educational Review* 9 (March 1939): 156–74; Willard Hogan, "The WPA Research and Records Program," *Harvard Educational Review* 13 (1943): 52–62.

25. Burton Folsom, Jr., *New Deal or Raw Deal? How FDR's Economic Legacy has Damaged America* (New York: Threshold, 2008); Amity Shlaes, *The Forgotten Man: A New History of the Great Depression* (New York: HarperCollins, 2007).

26. Eric Foner, *Give Me Liberty! An American History*, 2nd ed., vol. 2 (New York: W. W. Norton, 2008); James Roark, et al., *The American Promise: A History of the United States*, 4th ed., vol. 2 (New York: Bedford/St. Martin's, 2008); Jeanne Boydston, et al., *Making a Nation: The United States and Its People*, combined vol. (Upper Saddle River, NJ: Pearson, 2004). David Goldfield, et al., *The American Journey*, combined ed., doesn't even mention the Fair Labor Standards Act in the index (Upper Saddle River, NJ: Pearson, 2007), although the term does appear on a timeline.

27 Stephen J. DeCanio, "Expectations and Business Confidence During the Great Depression," in Barry N. Siegel, ed., *Money in Crisis: The Federal Reserve, the Economy, and Monetary Reform* (San Francisco: Pacific Institute, 1984), 157–75 (quotation on 167).

28. DeCanio, "Expectations and Business Confidence," 175.

29. Randall E. Parker, *The Economics of the Great Depression: A Twenty-First Century Look Back at the Economics of the Interwar Era* (Cheltenham, UK: Edward Elgar, 2007), 55–57.

30. Hopkins quoted in David Goldfield, et al., *The American Journey*, combined ed. (Upper Saddle River, NJ: Prentice-Hall, 1998), 830.

31. *New York Times*, October 24, 1935.

32. Harold Ickes, *The Secret Diary of Harold Ickes*, 3 vols. (New York: Simon & Schuster, 1954), 2:282–83.

33. Eugene Gerhart, *America's Advocate: Robert H. Jackson* (Indianapolis, IN: Bobbs-Merrill, 1958), 125–27.

34. Arthur Schlesinger, Jr., *The Age of Roosevelt: The Coming of the New Deal* (Boston: Houghton Mifflin, 1959), 308.

35. David C. John, "How to Fix Social Security," Heritage Foundation "Backgrounder," #1811, November 17, 2004.

36. Franklin D. Roosevelt's Message to Congress on Social Security, January 17, 1935, http://www.pbs.org/wgbh/amex/presidents/32_f_roosevelt/psources/ps_socsecspeech.html.

37. Franklin D. Roosevelt's Message to Congress on Social Security, January 17, 1935, http://www.pbs.org/wgbh/amex/presidents/32_f_roosevelt/psources/ps_socsecspeech.html.

38. Neal Boortz and John Lindner, *The Fair Tax Book: Saying Goodbye to the Income Tax and the IRS* (New York: Harper, 2006), 127.

39. Michael B. Katz, *In the Shadow of the Poorhouse: A Social History of Welfare in the United States*, 2nd ed. (New York: Basic Books, 1996), 133.

40. Charles Murray, *Losing Ground: American Social Policy, 1950–1980* (New York: Free Press, 1984).

41. Steve Sailer, "Black Illegitimacy Rate Declines," June 27, 2003, http://www.isteve.com/2003_Black_Illegitimacy_Rate_Declines.htm.

42. "Martin Van Buren has a Nightmare... And Gives Us Big Government in 1820," in Larry Schweikart, *Seven Events that Made America America* (New York: Sentinel, 2010).

43. Paul Johnson, *A History of the American People* (New York: HarperCollins, 1997), 501.

44. Jim Couch and William Shugart, *The Political Economy of the New Deal* (Northampton, MA: Edward Elgar, 1998).

45. Folsom, *New Deal or Raw Deal?*, 170.

46. Ibid.

Charles R. Kesler

The New New Deal

In President Obama, conservatives face the most formidable liberal politician in at least a generation. In 2008, he won the presidency with a majority of the popular vote—something a Democrat had not done since Jimmy Carter's squeaker in 1976—and handily increased the Democrats' control of both houses of Congress. Measured against roughly two centuries worth of presidential victories by Democratic nonincumbents, his win as a percentage of the popular vote comes in third behind FDR's in 1932 and Andrew Jackson's in 1828.

More important, Obama won the election not as a status quo liberal, but as an ambitious reformer. Far from being content with incremental gains, he set his sights on major systemic change in health care, energy and environmental policy, taxation, financial regulation, education, and even immigration, all pursued as elements of a grand strategy to "remake America." In other words, he longs to be another FDR, building a New New Deal for the twenty-first century, dictating the politics of his age, and enshrining the Democrats as the new majority party for several decades to come. Suddenly, the era of big government being over is over; and tax-and-spend liberalism is back with a vengeance. We face a $1.4 trillion federal deficit this fiscal year alone and

$10 to 12 trillion in total debt over the coming decade. If the ongoing expansion of government succeeds, there will also be very real costs to American freedom and to the American character. The Reagan Revolution is in danger of being swamped by the Obama Revolution.

To unsuspecting conservatives who had forgotten or never known what full-throated liberalism looked like before the Age of Reagan, Obama's eruption onto the scene came as a shock. And in some respects, obviously, he is a new political phenomenon. But in most respects, Obama does not represent something new under the sun. On the contrary, he embodies a rejuvenated and a repackaged version of something older than our grandmothers—namely the intellectual and social impulses behind modern liberalism. Yet even as President Obama stands victorious on health care and sets his sights on other issues, his popularity and that of his measures has tumbled. His legislative victories have been eked out on repeated party line votes of a sort never seen in the contests over Social Security, Medicare, and previous liberal policy successes, which were broadly popular and bipartisan. In short, a strange thing is happening on the way to liberal renewal. The closer liberalism comes to triumphing, the less popular it becomes. According to Gallup, 40 percent of Americans now describe themselves as conservative, 35 percent as moderates, and only 21 percent call themselves liberal. After one of its greatest triumphs in several generations, liberalism finds itself in an unexpected crisis—and a crisis that is not merely, as we shall see, a crisis of public confidence.

To try to understand better the difficulties in which the New New Deal finds itself, it might be useful to compare it to the original. The term itself, New Deal, was an amalgam of Woodrow Wilson's New Freedom and Teddy Roosevelt's Square Deal, and was deliberately ambiguous as to its meaning. It could mean the same game but with a new deal of the cards; or it could mean a wholly new game with new rules, that is, a new social contract for all of America. In effect, I think, the term's meaning was somewhere in between. But FDR liked to use the more conservative or modest sense of the term to disguise the more radical and ambitious ends that he was pursuing.

In its own time, the New Deal was extremely popular. Among its novel elements was a new kind of economic rights. The Progressives at the turn of the century had grown nervous over the closing of the American frontier and the rise of large corporations—developments they thought threatened the common man's equality of opportunity. Aside from antitrust efforts and wartime taxation, however, the Progressives did not get very far toward a redistributive agenda, and were actually wary of proclaiming new-fangled rights. They were more comfortable with duties than rights, and disapproved of the selfish penumbras cast by the natural rights doctrines of old. Woodrow Wilson and Teddy Roosevelt preached moral uplift—doing your duty in a more socialized or socialistic era. They tended to associate rights talk with individualism of the backward-looking sort. It took the cleverness of FDR and his advisors to figure out how rights could be adapted to promote bigger government and to roll back the old regime of individualism and limited government.

What was this new concept of rights? Instead of rights springing from the individual—as God-given aspects of our nature—FDR and the New Dealers conceived of individualism as springing from a kind of rights created by the state. These were social and economic rights, which FDR first proclaimed in his campaign speeches in 1932, kept talking about throughout the New Deal, and summed up toward the end of his life in his annual message to Congress in 1944. These were the kinds of rights that the New Deal especially promoted: the right to a job, the right to a decent home, the right to sell your agricultural products at a price that would allow you to keep your farm, the right to medical care, the right to vacations from work, and so on. FDR elevated these rights to be parts of what he called "our new constitutional order."

Of course, not all of these rights were enshrined in law. After all, President Obama has only just now enshrined a dubious right to health care into law. And not one of these rights was actually added to the Constitution, despite Roosevelt's pitching them as what he called a "second Bill of Rights." The fact that none of them was ever formulated into a constitutional amendment is entirely consistent with FDR's and modern liberals' belief in a living constitution—that is, a constitution that is changeable, Darwinian, not frozen in time, but rather creative and continually growing. Once upon a time, the growth and the conduct of government were severely restricted because a lot of liberal policies were thought to be unconstitutional. In fact, many New Deal measures proposed by FDR were struck down as unconstitutional by the Supreme Court in the 1930s. But nowadays it is hard to think of a measure expanding government power over private property and enterprise that the Court, much less Congress, would dismiss out of hand as simply unconstitutional.

If you consider the financial bailouts or the rewriting of bankruptcy law involved in the GM and Chrysler deals, these are the kinds of things that politicians in sounder times would have screamed bloody murder about as totally unconstitutional and illegal. But hardly a peep was heard. After all, once we have a living constitution, we shouldn't be surprised to find we have a living bankruptcy law, too. The meaning of the law can change overnight as circumstances dictate—or as the political reading of circumstances dictates.

Despite not being formally enshrined in the Constitution, most of these new rights—what we have come to call entitlement rights—did get added to the small "c" constitution of American politics anyway, either during the New Deal or during its sequel, the Great Society. Social Security, Medicare, Medicaid, and kindred welfare state programs moved to the center of our political life, dominating the domestic agenda and eventually usurping the majority of federal spending, now delicately termed "uncontrollable."

The social and economic rights inherent in these entitlements purported to make Americans secure, or at least to make them feel secure. "Necessitous men are not free men," FDR liked to say—which meant that freedom required government to take care of a person's necessities so that he might live comfortably, fearlessly, beyond necessity. The long-term problem with this was that the reasons given to justify the relatively modest initial welfare rights pointed far beyond themselves. No one ever doubted, for instance, that good houses, well-paying jobs, and decent medical care were fine things. But the liberal alchemy that transformed these fine things into "rights" was powerful magic. Such rights implied, in turn, duties to provide the houses, jobs, and medical care now guaranteed to most everyone.

And on whom did the duties fall? Liberalism never came clean on that question. It pointed sometimes to the rich, suggesting that enough of their wealth could be redistributed to provide the plenty that would be required to supply houses and medical care and jobs to those who lack them. But liberalism also liked to say that the duty to provide these things fell broadly upon the American middle class—that these were basically insurance programs into which people paid and from which they took out their benefits when needed.

Could future benefits be cut or eliminated? Liberals breathed nary a word about such unhappy scenarios, selling the new rights as though they were self-financing—that is, as if they would be cost-free in the long-term, if not a net revenue generator. In fact, entitlements are the offspring of formulas that can be trimmed or repealed by simple majorities of the legislature. And the benefits have to be paid for by someone—as it turns out, primarily by the young and the middle class.

The moral costs of the new rights went further. Virtue was the way that free people used to deal with their necessities. It took industry, frugality, and responsibility, for example, to go to work every morning to provide for your family. It took courage to handle the fears that inevitably come with life, especially in old age. But the new social and economic rights tended to undercut such virtues, subtly encouraging men and women to look to the government to provide for their needs and then to celebrate that dependency as if it were true freedom. In truth, the appetite for the stream of benefits promised by the new rights was more like an addiction, destructive of both freedom and virtue.

The new entitlements pointed to a beguiling version of the social contract. As FDR once described it, the new social contract calls for the people to consent to greater government power in exchange for the government providing them with rights: Social Security, Medicare, Medicaid, Obamacare, etc. The more power the people give government, the more rights we receive. FDR's New Deal implied that there is nothing to fear from making government bigger and bigger, because political tyranny—at least among advanced nations—is a thing of the past.

In truth, however, the new socioeconomic rights were group rights, not individual rights. They were rights for organized interests: labor unions, farmers, school teachers, old people, blacks, sick people, and so forth. Collectively, these rights encouraged citizens to think of themselves as members of pressure groups or to organize themselves into pressure groups. Subtly and not so subtly, citizens were taught to identify their rights with group self-interests of one kind or another.

These new group rights were conspicuously not attached to obligations. The old rights—the individual rights of the Declaration of Independence and the Constitution—had come bound up with duties. The right to life or the right to liberty implied a duty not to take away someone else's life or someone else's liberty. The new rights, on the other hand, had no corresponding duties—except perhaps to pay your taxes. The new rights pointed to a kind of moral anarchy in which rights without obligations became the currency of the realm—in which rights, understood as putative claims on resources, were effectively limited only by other, stronger such claims. The result was, at best, an equilibrium of countervailing power.

President Obama's New New Deal doesn't look so distinctive when you view it in this historical light. The collectivization of health care, for instance, is a hearty perennial of liberal politics and fulfills a 65-year-old promise made by FDR. Moreover, in cultivating the aura of a prophet-leader, uniquely fit to seize the historical moment and remake his country, Obama follows the theory and example of Woodrow Wilson. But there are signs of a few new or distinctive principles in this current leftward lurch, and I will mention two.

First, there is the postmodernism that crops up here and there. Postmodernism insists that there is no truth "out there" by which men can guide their thoughts and actions. Postmodern liberals admit, then, that there is no objective support—no support in nature or in God or in anything outside of our wills—for liberalism itself. Liberalism in these terms is just a preference. The leading academic postmodernist, the late Richard Rorty, argued that liberals are moral relativists who feel an "aversion to cruelty," and it is that aversion that makes them liberals. And indeed, if one admits that all moral principles are relative, the only thing that really sets one apart as a liberal is a certain kind of passion or feeling. President Obama calls this feeling empathy. And yes, of course, all this implies that conservatives don't have feelings for their fellow human beings—except perhaps a desire to be cruel to them.

Now I don't mean to suggest here that President Obama is a thoroughgoing postmodernist, because he is not. But neither is he just an old-fashioned progressive liberal of the 1930s variety. New Deal liberals believed in the future. In fact, they believed in a kind of predictive science of the future. Postmodernists reject all truth, including any assertions about progress or science. Postmodernists speak of narrative—one of those words one hears a lot of these days in politics—rather than truth. Narrative means something like this: Even if we can't find meaning in any kind of objective reality out there, we can still create meaning by telling each other stories, by constructing our own narratives—and the more inclusive and empathetic these narratives, the better. President Obama often speaks this postmodern language. For example, here is part of a discussion of the Constitution and the Declaration of Independence in his book, *The Audacity of Hope*:

> Implicit in [the Constitution's] structure, in the very idea of ordered liberty, was a rejection of absolute truth, the infallibility of any idea or ideology or theology or "ism," any tyrannical consistency that might lock future generations into a single, unalterable course, or drive both majorities and minorities into the cruelties [notice cruelty: he is against it] of the Inquisition, the pogrom, the gulag, or the jihad.

Obama's point here is that absolute truth and ordered liberty are incompatible, because absolute truth turns its believers into fanatics or moral monsters. Now granted, it was certainly a good thing that America escaped religious fanaticism and political tyranny. But no previous president ever credited these achievements to the Founders' supposed rejection of absolute truth—previously known simply as truth. What then becomes of those great self-evident truths that President Obama's admitted hero, Abraham Lincoln, celebrated and risked all to preserve? And that Martin Luther King, Jr., invoked so dramatically?

Postmodernism came out of the 1960s university—though it flowered, if that is the right word, in subsequent decades, especially after the collapse of Communism. President Obama is a child of the 1960s—born in 1961. The Sixties Left was in some ways strikingly different from the Thirties Left. For one thing, the '60s left was much more—as they liked to say in those days—"existentialist." That is, '60s leftists admitted to themselves that all values are relative, and therefore irrational. But they still believed or hoped that morality could be felt, or experienced through the feelings of a generation united in its demands for justice now. Shared feelings about values became a kind of substitute for truth among protesting liberals in the '60s, which goes far to explaining the emotionalism of liberals then and since. But when the country refused to second their emotions—when the country elected President Nixon in 1968 and again, by larger margins, in 1972—the kids grew bitter and increasingly alienated from the cause of democratic reform, which used to be liberalism's stock-in-trade. In this context, President Obama represents not only a return to a vigorous liberal reform agenda like the New Deal, but also a kind of bridge between the alienated campus left and the political left.

The second new element in President Obama's liberalism is even more striking than its postmodernism. It is how uncomfortable he is with American exceptionalism—and thus with America itself. President Obama considers this country deeply flawed from its very beginnings. He means not simply that slavery and other kinds of fundamental injustice existed, which everyone would admit. He means that the Declaration of Independence, when it said that all men are created equal, did not mean to include blacks or anyone else who is not a property-holding, white, European male—an argument put forward infamously by Chief Justice Roger Taney in the *Dred Scott* decision, and one that was powerfully refuted by Abraham Lincoln.

In short, President Obama agrees with his former minister, Reverend Jeremiah Wright, much more than he let on as a presidential candidate. Read closely, his famous speech on that subject in March 2008 doesn't hide his conclusion that Wright was correct—that America is a racist and ungodly country (hence, not "God Bless America," but "God Damn America!"). Obama agrees with Wright that in its origin, and for most of its history, America was racist, sexist, and in various ways vicious. Wright's mistake, Obama said, was underestimating America's capacity for change—a change strikingly illustrated by Obama's own advances and his later election. For Obama, Wright's mistake turned on not what America was, but what America could become—especially after the growth of liberalism in our politics in the course of the twentieth century. It was only liberalism that finally made America into a decent country, whereas for most of its history it was detestable.

Unlike most Americans, President Obama still bristles at any suggestion that our nation is better or even luckier than other nations. To be blunt, he despises the notion that Americans consider themselves special among the peoples of the world. This strikes him as the worst sort of ignorance and ethnocentrism, which is why it was so difficult for him to decide to wear an American flag lapel pin when he started running for president, even though he knew it was political suicide to refuse wearing it.

As President Obama hinted in his Berlin speech during the campaign, he really thinks of himself as a multiculturalist, as a citizen of the world, first, and only incidentally as an American. To put it differently, he regards patriotism as morally and intellectually inferior to cosmopolitanism. And, of course, he is never so much a citizen of the world as when defending the world's environment against mankind's depredations, and perhaps especially America's depredations. In general, the emotionalist defense of the earth—think of Al Gore—is now a vital part of the liberalism of our day. It is a kind of substitute for earlier liberals' belief in progress. Although his own election—and secondarily liberalism's achievements over the past century or so—help to redeem America in his view, Obama remains, in many ways, profoundly disconnected from his own land.

This is a very different state of mind and character from that of Franklin Roosevelt, who was the kind of progressive who thought that America was precisely the vanguard of moral progress in the world. This was the way Woodrow Wilson, Lyndon Johnson, and every great liberal captain before Obama thought about his country—as a profoundly moral force in the world, leading the nations of the world toward a better and more moral end point. Obama doesn't think that way, and therefore his mantle as an American popular leader—despite his flights of oratorical prowess—doesn't quite fit him in the way that FDR's fit him. One can see this in the tinges of irony that creep into Obama's rhetoric now and then—the sense that even he doesn't quite believe what he is saying; and he knows that but hopes that you don't.

Obama's ambivalence is, in many ways, the perfect symbol of the dilemma of the contemporary liberal. How can Obama argue that America and liberalism reject absolute truths, and in the same breath affirm—as he did recently to the United Nations—that human rights are self-evidently true? You can't have it both ways, though he desperately wants and tries to. Here, surely, is the deepest crisis of twentieth-century American liberalism—that it can no longer understand, or defend, its principles as true anymore. It knows that, but knows as well that to say so would doom it politically. Liberals are increasingly left with an amoral pragmatism that is hard to justify to themselves, much less to the American public. The problem for liberals today is that they risk becoming confidence men, and nothing but confidence men.

LUDWIG VON MISES

EXCERPTS FROM

ECONOMIC FREEDOM
AND INTERVENTIONISM

The Economic Role of Saving and Capital Goods

This article appeared in The Freeman, *August 1963.*

As the popular philosophy of the common man sees it, human wealth and welfare are the products of the cooperation of two primordial factors: nature and human labor. All the things that enable man to live and to enjoy life are supplied either by nature or by work or by a combination of nature-given opportunities with human labor. As nature dispenses its gifts gratuitously, it follows that all the final fruits of production, the consumers' goods, ought to be allotted exclusively to the workers whose toil has created them. But unfortunately in this sinful world conditions are different. There the "predatory" classes of the "exploiters" want to reap although they have not sown. The landowners, the capitalists, and the entrepreneurs appropriate to themselves what by rights belongs to the workers who have produced it. All the evils of the world are the necessary effect of this originary wrong.

Such are the ideas that dominate the thinking of most of our contemporaries. The socialists and the syndicalists conclude that in order to render human affairs more satisfactory it is necessary to eliminate

Ludwig von Mises, *Economic Freedom and Interventionism*, 3rd ed. (Indianapolis, IN: Liberty Fund, Inc., 2006), chapters 4, 16, 17, 20 & 31. See also the Ludwig von Mises Institute—http://mises.org.

those whom their jargon calls the "robber barons," i.e., the entrepreneurs, the capitalists, and the landowners, entirely; the conduct of all
production affairs ought to be entrusted either to the social apparatus of
compulsion and coercion, the state (in the Marxian terminology called
Society), or to the men employed in the individual plants or branches
of production.

Other people are more considerate in their reformist zeal. They do
not intend to expropriate those whom they call the "leisure class" entirely.
They want only to take away from them as much as is needed to bring
about "more equality" in the "distribution" of wealth and income.

But both groups, the party of the thoroughgoing socialists and that
of the more cautious reformers, agree on the basic doctrine according to
which profit and interest are "unearned" income and therefore, morally
objectionable. Both groups agree that profit and interest are the cause
of the misery of the great majority of all honest workingmen and their
families, and, in a decent and satisfactory organization of society, ought
to be sharply curbed, if not entirely abolished.

Yet this whole interpretation of human conditions is fallacious.
The policies engendered by it are pernicious from whatever point of
view we may judge them. Western civilization is doomed if we do not
succeed very soon in substituting reasonable methods of dealing with
economic problems for the present disastrous methods.

Three Factors of Production

Mere work—that is, effort not guided by a rational plan and not aided
by the employment of tools and intermediary products—brings about
very little for the improvement of the worker's condition. Such work is
not a specifically human device. It is what man has in common with all
other animals. It is bestirring oneself instinctively and using one's bare
hands to gather whatever is eatable and drinkable that can be found
and appropriated.

Physical exertion turns into a factor of human production when
it is directed by reason toward a definite end and employs tools and
previously produced intermediary products. Mind—reason—is the most
important equipment of man. In the human sphere, labor counts only

as *one* item in a combination of natural resources, capital goods, and labor; all these three factors are employed, according to a definite plan devised by reason, for the attainment of an end chosen. Labor, in the sense in which this term is used in dealing with human affairs, is only one of several factors of production.

The establishment of this fact demolishes entirely all the theses and claims of the popular doctrine of exploitation. Those saving and thereby accumulating capital goods, and those abstaining from the consumption of previously accumulated capital goods, contribute their share to the outcome of the processes of production. Equally indispensable in the conduct of affairs is the role played by the human mind. Entrepreneurial judgment directs the toil of the workers and the employment of the capital goods toward the ultimate end of production, the best possible removal of what causes people to feel discontented and unhappy.

What distinguishes contemporary life in the countries of Western civilization from conditions as they prevailed in earlier ages—and still exist for the greater number of those living today—is not the changes in the supply of labor and the skill of the workers and not the familiarity with the exploits of pure science and their utilization by the applied sciences, by technology. It is the amount of capital accumulated. The issue has been intentionally obscured by the verbiage employed by the international and national government agencies dealing with what is called foreign aid for the underdeveloped countries. What these poor countries need in order to adopt the Western methods of mass production for the satisfaction of the wants of the masses is not information about a "know how." There is no secrecy about technological methods. They are taught at the technological schools and they are accurately described in textbooks, manuals, and periodical magazines. There are many experienced specialists available for the execution of every project that one may find practicable for these backward countries. What prevents a country like India from adopting the American methods of industry is the paucity of its supply of capital goods. As the Indian government's confiscatory policies are deterring foreign capitalists from investing in India and as its prosocialist bigotry sabotages domestic accumulation of capital, their country depends on the alms that Western nations are giving to it.

Consumers Direct the Use of Capital

Capital goods come into existence by saving. A part of the goods produced is withheld from immediate consumption and employed for processes the fruits of which will only mature at a later date. All material civilization is based upon this "capitalistic" approach to the problems of production.

"Roundabout methods of production," as Böhm-Bawerk* called them, are chosen because they generate a higher output per unit of input. Early man lived from hand to mouth. Civilized man produces tools and intermediary products in the pursuit of long-range designs that finally bring forth results which direct, less time-consuming methods could never have attained, or could have attained only with an incomparably higher expenditure of labor and material factors,

Those saving—that is consuming less than their share of the goods produced—inaugurate progress toward general prosperity. The seed they have sown enriches not only themselves but also all other strata of society. It benefits the consumers.

The capital goods are for the owner a dead fund, a liability rather than an asset, if not used in production for the best possible and cheapest provision of the people with the goods and services they are asking for most urgently. In the market economy the owners of capital goods are forced to employ their property as if it were entrusted to them by the consumers under the stipulation to invest it in those lines in which it best serves those consumers. The capitalists are virtually mandataries of the consumers, bound to comply with their wishes.

In order to attend to the orders received from the consumers, their real bosses, the capitalists themselves must either themselves proceed to investment and the conduct of business or, if they are not prepared for such entrepreneurial activity or distrust their own abilities, hand over their funds to men whom they consider as better fitted for such a

---

*Eugen von Böhm-Bawerk (1851–1914), Austrian economist, professor to Ludwig von Mises, renowned for his scholarly study of interest theory, *Capital and Interest*. Böhm-Bawerk also served as Finance Minister in the Austro-Hungarian government, 1895, 1897, and 1900–1904.

function. Whatever alternative they may choose, the supremacy of the consumers remains intact. No matter what the financial structure of the firm or company may be, the entrepreneur who operates with other people's money depends no less on the market, that is, the consumers, than the entrepreneur who fully owns his outfit.

There is no other method to make wage rates rise than by investing more capital per worker. More investment of capital means: to give to the laborer more efficient tools. With the aid of better tools and machines, the quantity of the products increases and their quality improves. As the employer consequently will be in a position to obtain from the consumers more for what the employee has produced in one hour of work, he is able—and, by the competition of other employers, forced—to pay a higher price for the man's work.

Intervention and Unemployment

As the labor union doctrine sees it, the wage increases that they are obtaining by what is euphemistically called "collective bargaining" are not to burden the buyers of the products but should be absorbed by the employers. The latter should cut down what in the eyes of the communists is called "unearned income," that is, interest on the capital invested and the profits derived from success in filling wants of the consumers that until then had remained unsatisfied. Thus the unions hope to transfer step by step all this allegedly "unearned income" from the pockets of the capitalists and entrepreneurs into those of the employees.

What really happens on the market is, however, very different. At the market price **m** of the product **p**, all those who were prepared to spend **m** for a unit of **p** could buy as much as they wanted. The total quantity of **p** produced and offered for sale was **s**. It was not larger than **s** because with such a larger quantity the price, in order to clear the market, would have to drop below **m** to **m-**. But at this price of **m-** the producers with the highest costs would suffer losses and would thereby be forced to stop producing **p**. These marginal producers likewise incur losses and are forced to discontinue producing **p** if the wage increase enforced by the union (or by a governmental minimum wage decree) causes an increase of production costs not compensated by a rise in the price of **m** to **m+**. The resulting restriction of production necessitates a reduction of the labor force. The outcome of the union's "victory" is the unemployment of a number of workers.

The result is the same if the employers are in a position to shift the increase in production costs fully to the consumers, without a drop in the quantity of **p** produced and sold. If the consumers are spending more for the purchase of **p**, they must cut down their buying of some other commodity **q**. Then the demand for **q** drops and brings about unemployment of a part of the men who were previously engaged in turning out **q**.

The union doctrine qualifies interest received by the owners of the capital invested in the enterprise as "unearned" and concludes that it could be abolished entirely or considerably shortened without any harm to the employees and the consumers. The rise in production costs caused by wage increases could therefore be borne by shortening the company's net earnings and a corresponding reduction of the dividends paid to the shareholders. The same idea, is at the bottom of the unions' claim that every increase in what they call productivity of labor (that is, the sum of the prices received for the total output divided by the number of man hours spent in its production) should be added to wages. Both methods mean confiscating for the benefit of the employees the whole or at least a considerable part of the returns on the capital provided by the saving of the capitalists. But what induces the capitalists to abstain from consuming their capital and to increase it by new saving is the fact that their forbearance is counterbalanced by the proceeds of their investments. If one deprives them of these proceeds, the only use they can make of the capital they own is to consume it and thus to inaugurate general progressive impoverishment.

The Only Sound Policy

What elevates the wage rates paid to the American workers above the rates paid in foreign countries is the fact that the investment of capital per worker is higher in this country than abroad. Saving, the accumulation of capital, has created and preserved up to now the high standard of living of the average American employee.

All the methods by which the federal government and the governments of the states, the political parties, and the unions are trying to improve the conditions of people anxious to earn wages and salaries are not only vain but directly pernicious. There is only one kind of policy that can effectively benefit the employees, namely, a policy that refrains from putting any obstacles in the way of further saving and accumulation of capital.

· · · ·

Full Employment and Monetary Policy
This article appeared in *National Review*, June 22, 1957.
©1957 by National Review, Inc., 215 Lexington Avenue,
New York, New York 10016. Reprinted by permission.

At the price determined in an unhampered market all those who consider it satisfactory can sell and all those who are prepared to pay it can buy. If commodities remain unsold, this is not due to their "unsalability" but to speculation on the part of their owners; they hold out because they expect that they will be able to sell later at a higher price.

It is different when the authorities try to influence the market by compulsion. If the government decrees and enforces minimum prices higher than the potential market prices, a part of the supply offered for sale at the official minimum price remains unsold. This fact is well known. Therefore, if a government wants to push the price of a commodity above the potential market price, it does not simply resort to the fixing of minimum prices. Rather it tries to reduce the quantity offered for sale on the market, for instance by purchasing and withholding a part of the supply available.

All this applies also to labor. At the wage rates determined in the labor market everybody who looks for a job can get it and everybody who wants to employ workers can hire them. In the unhampered labor market, wage rates always tend toward full employment.

Market wage rates rise when the marginal productivity of labor outruns the marginal productivity of capital goods; or, more simply, when the per-head quota of capital invested increases. This is effected either by accumulation of new capital or by a drop in the number of workers. An increase in the amount of capital is the result of saving and consequent investment. A reduction in the supply of labor on the market can be brought about by restricting immigration. In the age of liberalism, in the traditional classical meaning of the term, there were practically no migration barriers. In this age of welfarism and unionism, well-nigh all governments have either completely prohibited immigration or, as for instance the United States and other American republics, stipulated definite quotas. Beyond that, some American unions have tried to reduce still more the number of jobseekers in their segments of the labor market by excluding racial minorities from some kinds of employment and by rendering entrance into certain branches extremely difficult.

There is need to emphasize that only such "artificial" or "institutional" reduction of the labor supply makes it possible for the unions to raise their members' wage rates. Their success in raising the wages of their members is won at the expense of those whom they have excluded. These outsiders are forced to look for jobs in industries in which remuneration is lower than what they would have earned in the field that is closed to them.

Effects of Labor Unions

Labor unionism as we know it today is the outcome of a long evolution. In the beginning only a few branches were organized, mostly those with the best-paid skilled workers. At that time, those who could not find a job in a unionized industry, because wages had been pushed above the potential market height and thereby the demand for labor had been reduced, were forced to go into the non-unionized branches of business. Their influx into these branches increased in them the number of jobseekers and thus tended to depress there the height of wage rates. Thus, the higher wages of unionized workers brought about pressures on the jobs and wages of non-unionized workers. The more unionization spread, the more difficult it became for those who had lost their jobs on account of union policy to find other jobs; they remained unemployed. Wherever and whenever the unions succeeded in raising wage rates above the potential market rate, i.e., above the amount the workers would have earned without union interference, "institutional" unemployment developed as a lasting phenomenon.

As the union leaders see it, the determination of wage rates is the outcome of a struggle for power between the employers and the employees. Their interpretation does not acknowledge that wages depend on the state of the market and that the workers who receive the wages form the immense majority of the consumers out of whose pockets the wages are ultimately paid. The average wage earner considers it unfair that the movie star and the boxing champion are paid a hundred times more than the welder and the charwoman. He fails to see that his own behavior, his own purchases on the market, and those of other wage earners like him contribute to this result. An entrepreneur cannot pay more to a worker than he expects to collect from the customers for this man's performance. Even the most infatuated supporters of the exploitation doctrine are finally forced to admit that, at a certain height of wage rates, lasting unemployment of a considerable part of the potential labor force becomes unavoidable.

The market economy is ultimately controlled by the conduct of the consumers, that is by the conduct of all the people. In buying or in desisting from buying, the consumers determine what ought to be produced, of what quality and in what quantity. They determine who should make profits and who should suffer losses. They make rich men poor and poor men rich. The consumers are continuously shifting control of the material factors of production into the hands of those entrepreneurs, capitalists, and landowners who are most successful in supplying them, the consumers, in the cheapest and best possible way. Thus, in the capitalistic economy control of the factors of production is, as it were, a revocable mandate granted by the public. The operation of the market, in a daily repeated plebiscite, assigns to everybody the place in which he is to contribute to the united effort of all. This daily plebiscite determines the height of everybody's income.

The Alternative—Socialism

The individual resents the fact that he is forced to adjust himself to the conditions of the market and must forgo many of his own wishes and inclinations. However, it is obvious that the immeasurable benefits that cooperation under the system of the social division of labor affords to everybody must be paid for by some sacrifices. Whatever society's economic organization may be, it must always prevent man from behaving without due concern for the existence of others. The alternative to the hegemony of the market under capitalism is not absolute freedom, but the unconditional surrender of all to the supremacy of the socialist planning authority.

Society cannot do without an institution that channels the available workers into those branches in which they are most urgently needed and withdraws them from those in which there is less need for them. The labor market serves this purpose in raising wage rates in expanding industries and reducing them in shrinking industries. The alternative is to assign to each man a job by government order.

The tyranny of the labor market is milder than that of socialist regimentation. It grants to the individual a margin within which he is free to ignore the market's directives. If he is prepared to put up with a lower income, he can choose vocations in which he can either dedicate himself to his ideals or indulge his inclination for laziness. But the command of the socialist dictator does not brook contradiction.

There is only one method to abolish lasting mass unemployment, the return to the freedom of the labor market. Lasting mass unemployment is always institutional. It is the inevitable effect of the enforcement of wage rates that are higher than the potential market rates at which all jobseekers could find employment. It does not matter whether these minimum wage rates were decreed directly by the government or induced indirectly by the fact that the government is not willing to protect the enterprises and the strikebreakers against the violence of the unions.

The political power of the unions has succeeded in suppressing the dispassionate discussion of these problems. But it could not prevent the undesirable consequences of the unions' policies from wreaking havoc. In the twenties, in many European countries mass unemployment became the main political embarrassment. It was clear that these conditions could not continue indefinitely. Something had to be done. Smart politicians thought that they had found a solution. As it was deemed impermissible to antagonize the unions, and to tamper with the money wage rates dictated by them, they resorted to currency devaluation, reducing purchasing power and, thus, real wage rates. England took the lead in 1931. Very soon other countries followed.

For a while the nostrum worked. Some time passed before the unions began to pay full attention to the drop in the monetary unit's purchasing power. But when the index of the cost of living became the main issue in wage negotiations, the monetary method of eliminating mass unemployment had exhausted its serviceableness.

A New Messiah

It was precisely at this juncture that Lord Keynes entered the scene with his good tidings, the allegedly new economic doctrine designed to supersede all previous economic teachings, including those of the earlier writings of Keynes himself. Following in the wake of the politicians who in 1931 had demolished the British gold standard, and of their imitators, he pointed out that "a gradual and automatic lowering of real wages," that results from a lowering of the monetary unit's purchasing power, will be less strongly resisted than attempts to revise money wages downward. But in 1936, when Keynes' book was published, this no longer agreed with the facts.

Keynes' *General Theory* of 1936 and his later writings are hardly different from the bulk of inflationist literature which for more than a century has flooded the world. Like the authors of all these pamphlets, Keynes tries to dispose of all those who do not share his opinions by calling them "orthodox." He never tries to disprove their teachings rationally. He enriched the prosaic language of diplomatic correspondence by terms borrowed from the messianic jargon of the "monetary cranks." For instance, in the British document that inaugurated the events which finally led to the establishment of the International Monetary Fund, he declared that credit expansion performs the "miracle . . . of turning a stone into bread." But he did not add any new idea to the old, long since entirely refuted and discredited arguments of the inflationists. All Keynes accomplished was to coin a new slogan—"full employment"—which became the motto of present-day policies of inflation and credit expansion.

The full-employment doctrine underlying these inflation and credit expansion policies, in complete accord with the teachings of the *Communist Manifesto*, declares that the very operation of the capitalistic mode of production inevitably generates the emergence of mass unemployment. Unlike the creed of the more consistent Marxians it does not, however, contend that the return of periods of economic depression and large-scale unemployment is absolutely inevitable in the market economy. It attributes to the State (with a capital S) the power to create jobs for everybody. All that the State has to do is to put more money into the hands of the people and thereby to increase demand. It is wrong, this official full-employment doctrine goes on to assert, to call an increase in the quantity of money created for this purpose, inflation. It is just "full-employment" policy. Those "reactionaries" who ramble on about monetary stability and the return to gold are depicted as the worst enemies of civilization, public welfare and the common man.

The climate of opinion of the United States is fully dominated by these ideas. The unions are in a position to succeed in what are euphemistically called wage negotiations because the laws are loaded in favor of the unions and because the Government is always prepared to use its power to their advantage. (In this regard it does not make much difference whether the Administration is Republican or Democratic.) From time to time the unions ask for raises; the employers are forced to yield; as soon as business begins to slacken and workers are discharged, public opinion vehemently asks for more "easy money." After a short period of hesitation the Administration gives in and puts pressure upon the Federal Reserve Board to reduce interest rates, so as to increase the quantity of money and make it "easier."

A Few Dissenters

Fortunately the inflationary policy is still seriously resisted by a group of critics who are not numerous but who are conspicuous by their competence and familiarity with the problems involved. Among these dissenters are several eminent writers, a few influential businessmen and, what is worthy of notice, also some members of the Federal Reserve Board. This handful of men do not have the power to put an end to this nefarious monetary and credit policy. Yet their weighty reasoning has in the last years, especially under President Eisenhower's regime, succeeded in keeping the inflationary ventures within narrow limits. It is the merit of their warning voices that the world's richest country has up to now not embarked upon the pernicious policy of runaway inflation.

The full significance of this success can only be appreciated if one takes into account the vehemence of the pro-inflationist propaganda of university teachers and of "progressive" politicians and journalists. Some of the utterances of these people are really amazing. Thus several years ago the then Chairman of the Federal Reserve Bank of New York declared: "Final freedom from the domestic money market exists for every sovereign national state where there exists an institution which functions in the manner of a modern central bank, and whose currency is not convertible into gold or into some other commodity." The lecture that contained this statement had the characteristic title: "Taxes For Revenue Are Obsolete." In the same vein, a professor of economics pointed out, in a voluminous work, that the government, "can raise all the money it needs by printing it"; the purpose of taxation is "never to raise money" but "to leave less in the hands of the taxpayer."

The weakness of the small group advocating sound monetary policy and fighting all inflationary measures is their disinclination to attack the "full employment" doctrine openly and directly. It is practically impossible to bring this issue up before the public. Certainly there are men with the courage to risk their careers or even their personal safety by criticizing the "full employment" doctrine. But there are neither newspapers nor publishers who would dare to spread doctrines that criticize and reject the institution of unionism in principle. Even those writers who occasionally expose blackmail and embezzlement on the part of individual union officers emphasize again and again that they consider the institution of unionism as such, and the policies of the unions, as beneficial to the welfare of the wage earners and the whole nation; they merely intend to free the unions from dishonest leaders. As long as such ideas about the effects of unionism prevail, even modest attempts at repealing the privileges granted to the unions by the New Deal are doomed to fail, and there cannot be any question of Protecting enterprises and those willing to work against violence on the part of the unions.

At the most recent meeting of the International Monetary Fund there was much talk about the danger of inflation. In order to fight this danger, it is no longer enough to work for a better understanding of monetary problems. It is no less important to enlighten public opinion about the absurdity of the "full-employment" doctrine that guides the conduct of all governments and all political parties today.

• • • •

Gold versus Paper

This article appeared in The Freeman, *July 13, 1953*

Most people take it for granted that the world will never return to the gold standard. The gold standard, they say, is as obsolete as the horse and buggy. The system of government-issued fiat money provides the treasury with the funds required for an open-handed spending policy that benefits everybody; it forces prices and wages up and the rate of interest down and thereby creates prosperity. It is a system that is here to stay.

Now whatever virtues one may ascribe—undeservedly—to the modern variety of the greenback standard, there is one thing that it certainly cannot achieve. It can never become a permanent, lasting system of monetary management. It can work only as long as people are not aware of the fact that the government plans to keep it.

The Alleged Blessings of Inflation

The alleged advantages that the champions of fiat money expect from the operation of the system they advocate are temporary only. An injection of a definite quantity of new money into the nation's economy starts a boom as it enhances prices. But once this new money has exhausted all its price-raising potentialities and all prices and wages are adjusted to the increased quantity of money in circulation, the stimulation it provided to business ceases. Thus even if we neglect dealing with the

undesired and undesirable consequences and social costs of such inflationary measures and, for the sake of argument, even if we accept all
that the harbingers of "expansionism" advance in favor of inflation,
we must realize that the alleged blessings of these policies are short-
lived. If one wants to perpetuate them, it is necessary to go on and on
increasing the quantity of money in circulation and expanding credit
at an ever-accelerated pace. But even then the ideal of the expansion-
ists and inflationists, viz., an everlasting boom not upset by any reverse,
could not materialize.

A fiat-money inflation can be carried on only as long as the masses
do not become aware of the fact that the government is committed to
such a policy. Once the common man finds out that the quantity of cir-
culating money will be increased more and more, and that consequently
its purchasing power will continually drop and prices will rise to ever
higher peaks, he begins to realize that the money in his pocket is melting
away. Then he adopts the conduct previously practiced only by those
smeared as profiteers; he "flees into real values." He buys commodities,
not for the sake of enjoying them, but in order to avoid the losses involved
in holding cash. The knell of the inflated monetary system sounds. We
have only to recall the many historical precedents beginning with the
Continental Currency of the War of Independence.

Why Perpetual Inflation Is Impossible

The fiat-money system, as it operates today in this country and in some
others, could avoid disaster only because a keen critique on the part of a
few economists alerted public opinion and forced upon the government
cautious restraint in their inflationary ventures. If it had not been for the
opposition of these authors, usually labeled orthodox and reactionary,
the dollar would long since have gone the way of the German mark
of 1923. The catastrophe of the Reich's currency was brought about
precisely because no such opposition was vocal in Weimar Germany.

Champions of the continuation of the easy money scheme are
mistaken when they think that the policies they advocate could prevent
altogether the adversities they complain about. It is certainly possible
to go on for a while in the expansionist routine of deficit spending by

borrowing from the commercial banks and supporting the government bond market. But after some time it will be imperative to stop. Otherwise the public will become alarmed about the future of the dollar's purchasing power and a panic will follow. As soon as one stops, however, all the unwelcome consequences of the aftermath of inflation will be experienced. The longer the preceding period of expansion has lasted, the more unpleasant those consequences will be.

The attitude of a great many people with regard to inflation is ambivalent. They are aware, on the one hand, of the dangers inherent in a continuation of the policy of pumping more and more money into the economic system. But as soon as anything substantial is done to stop increasing the amount of money, they begin to cry out about high interest rates and bearish conditions on the stock and commodity exchanges. They are loath to relinquish the cherished illusion which ascribes to government and central banks the magic power to make people happy by endless spending and inflation.

Full Employment and the Gold Standard

The main argument advanced today against the return to the gold standard is crystallized in the slogan "full-employment policy." It is said that the gold standard paralyzes efforts to make unemployment disappear.

On a free labor market the tendency prevails to fix wage rates for every kind of work at such a height that all employers ready to pay these wages find all the employees they want to hire, and all job-seekers ready to work for these wages find employment. But if compulsion or coercion on the part of the government or the labor unions is used to keep wage rates above the height of these market rates, unemployment of a part of the potential labor force inevitably results.

Neither governments nor labor unions have the power to raise wage rates for all those eager to find jobs. All they can achieve is to raise wage rates for the workers employed, while an increasing number of people who would like to work cannot get employment. A rise in the market wage rate—i.e., the rate at which all job-seekers finally find employment—can be brought about only by raising the marginal productivity of labor. Practically, this means by raising the per-capita quota of capital invested. Wage rates and standards of living are much higher today than they were in the past because under capitalism the increase in capital invested by far exceeds the increase in population. Wage rates in the United States are many times higher than in India because the American per-capita quota of capital invested is many times higher than the Indian per-capita quota of capital invested.

There is only one method for a successful "full-employment policy"—let the market determine the height of wage rates. The method that Lord Keynes has baptized "full-employment policy" also aimed at re-establishment of the rate which the free labor market tends to fix. The peculiarity of Keynes' proposal consisted in the fact that it proposed to eradicate the discrepancy between the decreed and enforced official wage rate and the potential rate of the free labor market by lowering the purchasing power of the monetary unit. It aimed at holding nominal wage rates, i.e., wage rates expressed in terms of the national fiat money, at the height fixed by the government's decree or by labor union pressure. But as the quantity of money in circulation was increased and consequently a trend toward a drop in the monetary unit's purchasing power developed, real wage rates, i.e., wage rates expressed in terms of commodities, would fall. Full employment would be reached when the difference between the official rate and the market rate of real wages disappeared.

There is no need to examine anew the question whether the Keynesian scheme could really work. Even if, for the sake of argument, we were to admit this, there would be no reason to adopt it. Its final effect upon the conditions of the labor market would not differ from that achieved by the operation of the market factors when left alone. But it attains this end only at the cost of a very serious disturbance in the whole price structure and thereby the entire economic system. The Keynesians refuse to call "inflation" any increase in the quantity of money in circulation that is designed to fight unemployment. But this is merely playing with words. For they themselves emphasize that the success of their plan depends on the emergence of a general rise in commodity prices.

It is, therefore, a fable that the Keynesian full-employment recipe could achieve anything for the benefit of the wage earners that could not be achieved under the gold standard. The full-employment argument is as illusory as all the other arguments advanced in favor of increasing the quantity of money in circulation.

The Specter of an Unfavorable
International Balance

A popular doctrine maintains that the gold standard cannot be preserved by a country with what is called an "unfavorable balance of payments." It is obvious that this argument is of no use to the American opponents of the gold standard. The United States [1953] has a very considerable surplus of exports over imports. This is neither an act of God nor an effect of wicked isolationism. It is the consequence of the fact that this country, under various titles and pretexts, gives financial aid to many foreign nations. These grants alone enable the foreign recipients to buy more in this country than they are selling in its markets. In the absence of such subsidies it would be impossible for any country to buy anything abroad that it could not pay for, either by exporting commodities or by rendering some other service such as carrying foreign goods in its ships or entertaining foreign tourists. No artifices of monetary policy, however sophisticated and however ruthlessly enforced by the police, can in any way alter this fact.

It is not true that the so-called have-not countries have derived any advantage from their abandonment of the gold standard. The virtual repudiation of their foreign debts, and the virtual expropriation of foreign investments that it involved, brought them no more than a momentary respite. The main and lasting effect of abandoning the gold standard, the disintegration of the international capital market, hit these debtor countries much harder than it hit the creditor countries. The falling off of foreign investments is one of the main causes of the calamities they are suffering today.

The gold standard did not collapse. Governments, anxious to spend, even if this meant spending their countries into bankruptcy, intentionally aimed at destroying it. They are committed to an anti-gold policy, but they have lamentably failed in their endeavors to discredit gold. Although officially banned, gold in the eyes of the people is still money, even the only genuine money. The more prestige the legal-tender notes produced by the various government printing offices enjoy, the more stable their exchange ratio is against gold. But people do not hoard paper; they hoard gold. The citizens of this country, of course, are not free to hold, to buy, or to sell gold.* If they were allowed to do so, they certainly would.

No international agreements, no diplomats, and no supernational bureaucracies are needed in order to restore sound monetary conditions. If a country adopts a non-inflationary policy and clings to it, then the condition required for the return to gold is already present. The return to gold does not depend on the fulfillment of some material condition. It is an ideological problem. It presupposes only one thing: the abandonment of the illusion that increasing the quantity of money creates prosperity.

The excellence of the gold standard is to be seen in the fact that it makes the monetary unit's purchasing power independent of the arbitrary and vacillating policies of governments, political parties, and pressure groups. Historical experience, especially in the last decades, has clearly shown the evils inherent in a national currency system that lacks this independence.

• • • •

Inflation: An Unworkable Fiscal Policy

Transcript of remarks before the Conference on the Economics of Mobilization, held at White Sulphur Springs, West Virginia, April 6–8, 1951, under the sponsorship of the University of Chicago Law School. Reprinted from The Commercial and Financial Chronicle, *April 26, 1951.*

In dealing with problems concerned with the economics of mobilization, it is first of all necessary to realize that fiscal policies have reached a turning point.

In recent decades all nations have looked upon the income and the wealth of the more prosperous citizens as an inexhaustible reserve

---

*This right to own gold was restored to U.S. citizens as of January 1, 1975.

which could be freely tapped. Whenever there was need for additional funds, one tried to collect them by raising the taxes to be paid by the upper-income brackets. There seemed to be enough money for any suggested expenditure because there seemed to be no harm in "soaking the rich" a bit more. As the votes of these rich do not count much in elections, the members of the legislative bodies were always ready to increase public spending at their expense. There is a French dictum: *Les affaires, c'est l'argent des autres.* "Business is other people's money." In these last 60 years political and fiscal affairs were virtually "other people's money." Let the rich pay, was the slogan.

End of an Era

Now this period of fiscal history has come to an end. With the exception of the United States and some of the British Dominions, what has been called the ability-to-pay of the wealthy citizens has been completely absorbed by taxes. No further funds of any significance can be collected from them. Henceforth all government spending will have to be financed by taxing the masses.

The European nations concerned are not yet fully aware of this fact because they have found a substitute. They are getting Marshall Plan aid; the U. S. taxpayer fills the gap.

In this country things have not yet gone as far as they have in other countries. It is still possible to raise an additional $2 or $3 billion, or perhaps even $4 billion, by increasing corporation taxes, and "excess profits" taxes, and by rendering the personal income tax more progressive. But under present conditions, even $4 billion would be only a fraction of what the Treasury needs. Thus, in this country we are also at the end of a period of fiscal policies. The whole philosophy of public finance must undergo a revision. In considering the pros and cons of a suggested expenditure the members of Congress will no longer be able to think: The rich have enough; let *them* pay. In the future, the voters on whose ballots the Congressmen depend will have to pay.

Inflation, an increase in money and credit, is certainly not a means to avoid or to postpone for more than a short time the need to resort to taxes levied on people other than those belonging to the rich minority.

If, for the sake of argument, we leave aside all the objections which may be raised against any inflationary policy, we must take into account the fact that inflation can never be more than a temporary makeshift. Inflation cannot be continued over a long period of time without defeating its fiscal purpose and ending in a complete debacle as was the case in this country with the Continental currency, in France with the *mandats territoriaux* and in Germany with the mark in 1923.

What makes it possible for a government to increase its funds by inflation is the ignorance of the public. The people must ignore the fact that the government has chosen inflation as a fiscal system and plans to go on with inflation endlessly. It must ascribe the general rise in prices to other causes than to the policy of the government and must assume that prices will drop again in a not-too-distant future. If this opinion fades away, inflation comes to a catastrophic breakdown.

The Housewife's Behavior

If the housewife who needs a new frying pan reasons: "Now prices are too high; I will postpone the purchase until they drop again," inflation can still fulfill its fiscal purpose. As long as people share this view, they increase their cash holdings and bank balances, and a part of the newly created money is absorbed by these additional cash holdings and bank balances; prices on the market do not rise in proportion to the inflation.

But then—sooner or later—comes a turning point. The housewife discovers that the government expects to go on inflating and that consequently prices will continue to rise more and more. Then she reasons: "I do not need a new frying pan today; I shall only need one next year. But I had better buy it now because next year the price will be much higher." If this insight spreads, inflation is done for, then all people rush to buy. Everybody is anxious to reduce his holding of cash because he does not want to be hurt by the drop in the monetary unit's purchasing power. The phenomenon then appears which, in Europe was called the "flight into real values." People rush to exchange their depreciating paper money for something tangible, something real. The knell sounds of the currency system involved.

In this country we have not yet reached this second and final stage of every protracted inflation. But if the authorities do not very soon abandon any further attempt to increase the amount of money in circulation and to expand credit, we shall one day come to the same unpleasant result. It is not a matter of choosing between financing the increased government expenditure by collecting taxes and borrowing from the public on the one hand and financing it by inflation on the other hand. Inflation can never be an instrument of fiscal policy over a long period of time. Continued inflation inevitably leads to catastrophe.

Therefore, we should not waste our time in discussing methods of price control. Price control cannot prevent the rise in prices if inflation is going on. Even capital punishment could not make price control work in the days of Emperor Diocletian or during the French Revolution. Let us concentrate our efforts on the problem of how to avoid inflation, not upon useless schemes of how to conceal its inexorable consequences.

Taxation the Key

What is needed in wartime is to divert production and consumption from peacetime channels toward military goals. In order to achieve this, it is necessary for the government to tax the citizens, to take away from them the money, which they would otherwise spend for things they must no longer buy and consume, so the government can spend it for the conduct of the war.

At the breakfast table of every citizen in wartime sits an invisible guest, as it were, a GI who shares his meal. Parked in the citizen's garage is not only the family car, but also—invisibly—a tank or a plane. The important fact is that a GI needs more in food, clothing, and other things than he used to consume as a civilian. And military equipment wears out much more quickly than civilian equipment. The costs of a modern war are enormous.

The adequate method of providing the funds the government needs for war is, of course, taxation. Part of the funds may also be provided by borrowing from the public, the citizens. But if the Treasury increases the amount of money in circulation or borrows from the commercial banks, it inflates. Inflation can do the job for a limited time.

But it is the most expensive method of financing a war; it is socially disruptive and should be avoided.

Inflation: A Convenient Makeshift

There is no need to dwell upon the disastrous consequences of inflation. All people agree in this regard. But inflation is a very convenient makeshift for those in power. It is a handy means to divert the resentment of the people from the government. In the eyes of the masses, big business, the "profiteers," the merchants—not the Administration—appear responsible for the rise in prices and the ensuing need to restrict consumption.

Perhaps somebody will consider what I am saying here as anti-democratic, reactionary, and economic royalism. But the truth is that inflation is a typically anti-democratic measure. It is a policy of governments that do not have the courage to tell the people honestly what the real costs of their conduct of affairs are.

A truly democratic government would have to tell the voters openly that they must pay higher taxes because expenses have risen considerably. But it is much more agreeable for a government to present only a part of the bill to the people and to resort to inflation for the rest of its expenditures. What a triumph if they can say: Everybody's income is rising, everybody has now more money in his pocket, business is booming.

Deficit spending is not a new invention. During the greater part of the 19th century it was the preferred fiscal method of precisely those governments that were not then considered democratic and progressive—Austria, Italy, and Russia. Austria's budget showed a deficit yearly from 1781 on, until the late '80s of the 19th century, when an orthodox professor of economics, Dunajewski, as Minister of Finance, restored the budgetary equilibrium. There is no reason to be proud of deficit spending, nor to call it progress.

Going After Lower Brackets

If one wants to collect more taxes, it will be necessary to lay a burden greater than hitherto on the lower income brackets, the strata of society whose members consume the much greater part of the total amount consumed in this country. Up to now it has been customary to tax predominantly corporations and individuals with higher incomes. But even the outright confiscation of these revenues would only cover a fraction of the additional funds the country needs today.

Some experts have declared that it is necessary to tax the people until it hurts. I disagree with these sadists. The purpose of taxation is not to hurt, but to raise the money the country needs to rearm and to fight in Korea. It is a sad fact that world affairs now make it necessary for the government to force people who used to buy nylon stockings and shirts to shift to other du Pont products, namely munitions.

In his book on *Eternal Peace*, the German philosopher Immanuel Kant (1724–1804) suggested that government should be forbidden to finance wars by borrowing. He expected that the warlike spirit would dwindle if all countries had to pay cash for their wars. However, no serious objection can be raised against borrowing from the public, from people who have saved and are prepared to invest in government bonds. But borrowing from the commercial banks is tantamount to printing additional bank notes and expanding the amount of deposits subject to check. That is inflation.

Semantic Confusion

There is nowadays a very reprehensible, even dangerous, semantic confusion that makes it extremely difficult for the non-expert to grasp the true state of affairs. Inflation, as this term was always used everywhere and especially in this country, means increasing the quantity of money and bank notes in circulation and the quantity of bank deposits subject to check. But people today use the term "inflation" to refer to the phenomenon that is an inevitable consequence of inflation, that is the tendency of all prices and wage rates to rise. The result of this deplorable confusion is that there is no term left to signify the cause of this rise in prices and wages. There is no longer any word available to signify the phenomenon that has been, up to now, called inflation. It follows that nobody cares about inflation in the traditional sense of the term. As you cannot talk about something that has no name, you cannot fight it. Those who pretend to fight inflation are in fact only fighting what is the inevitable consequence of inflation, rising prices. Their ventures are doomed to failure because they do not attack the root of the evil. They try to keep prices low while firmly committed to a policy of increasing the quantity of money that must necessarily make them soar. As long as this technological confusion is not entirely wiped out, there cannot be any question of stopping inflation.

Look at the silly term, "inflationary pressures." There is no such thing as an "inflationary pressure." There is inflation or there is the absence of inflation. If there is no increase in the quantity of money and if there is no credit expansion, the average height of prices and wages will by and large remain unchanged. But if the quantity of money and credit is increased, prices and wages must rise, whatever the government may decree. If there is no inflation, price control is superfluous. If there is inflation, price control is a sham, a hopeless venture.

It is the government that makes our inflation. The policy of the Treasury, and nothing else.

We have been told a lot about the need for, and the virtues of, direct controls.

We have learned that they preserve the individual's liberty to choose the grocer he prefers. I do not want to examine what value may be attached to direct controls from a metaphysical point of view. I only want to stress *one* fact: As a means for preventing and fighting inflation or its consequences, direct controls are absolutely useless.

• • • •

Professor Hutt on Keynesianism
This article appeared in *The Freeman*, January 1964.

The Keynesian doctrine as developed by 1936 in *The General Theory of Unemployment, Interest, and Money*, tries to prove the soundness of the two most popular but least tenable components of contemporary economic policies: inflationism and labor unionism. At the time of its publication the spectacular failure of these two methods of interfering with the market phenomena could no longer be concealed. Yet the governments and the political parties were firmly resolved not to abandon "deficit spending" and the support of labor union violence and intimidation. Their official wisdom explained the progressive rise in prices—which they misnamed inflation—as caused by machinations on the part of bad people, the profiteers, and they considered that unemployment was one of the unavoidable shortcomings of a "free," i.e., not regimented, economy.

But from day to day it became more obvious that it was not enough to find a lame excuse for the current policies. What the noncommunist West seemed to need was a comprehensive doctrine that could be adopted as the economic philosophy of these governments that, while ostensibly proclaiming their anticommunism, step by step approached a system of all-round government control of business. *The General Theory's* success was due to the fact that it tried to provide such a justification of the American New Deal and the devaluation practices of the various European nations.

The enthusiastic praise that Keynes' doctrine received on the part of professors and authors propagating government omnipotence could for a while divert attention from the fact that from the beginning all discriminating economists rejected it and unmasked its inherent fallacies. Some of the most important of these critical essays were collected and republished by Henry Hazlitt under the title *The Critics of Keynesian Economics* (Van Nostrand, 1960). Hazlitt himself has in a voluminous brilliantly written study, *The Failure of the "New Economics"* (Van Nostrand, 1959), clearly demonstrated the shortcomings, contradictions, and other failings of Keynesianism.

To Clear the Air

As an economic doctrine, Keynesianism is now dead. But the serious errors and misunderstandings of fundamental issues of economics that made its emergence and its fleeting success possible still prevail. There remain with us many empty slogans and illusory concepts that easily mislead those seeking a satisfactory interpretation of phenomena. It is necessary to clear away the debris of the Keynesian structure in order to open the way for a correct grasp of the principles of the market and the functioning of price flexibility.

This is the task that the new book of Professor W. H. Hutt, *Keynesianism—Retrospect and Prospect* (Chicago: Regnery, 1963, 447 pp.), wants to accomplish. Hutt calls his work *A Critical Restatement of Basic Economic Principles*. Such a restatement was badly needed indeed. The main failure of Keynes and all his disciples and admirers is to be seen in the fact that they simply do not know what prices are, how they originate, and what they bring about.

Prices come into existence by the eagerness of people to exchange one commodity or service against another commodity or service. They are the outcome of various individuals' readiness to buy or to sell. Every price is the outgrowth of a definite constellation of demand and supply. No price could ever be different from what it really was, because people failed to appear on the market at that time who were ready to bid a higher price, or who were ready to ask a lower price. The structure of prices reflects the state of the material conditions determining people's existence and the success of the endeavors made to satisfy the most urgent needs, as far as these material conditions make it feasible.

Prices cannot be manipulated *ad libitum* [at will] by the social apparatus of coercion and compulsion, the police power. All the government—or a labor union to which the government has virtually delegated its power of enforcing orders by violent action—can achieve is to substitute coercion for voluntary action. Where there is coercion, the market economy no longer functions; disorder results in the production and the marketing of the articles subject to the governmental decree. Then the spokesmen of the authorities point to the inefficiency of the market system and ask for more government meddling with the price system.

The Market Economy

Professor Hutt analyzes point by point all the alleged shortcomings of the free market about which people complain. He presents a comprehensive analysis of all aspects of the Keynesian interpretation of the market economy. Most of the rising generation of economists were taught Keynesianism and therefore ignore all that economic theory has brought forward for an elucidation of what is going on in production and in the marketing of the products. A careful study of Professor Hutt's new volume will lead them back to a correct grasp of the problems of the market economy.

Professor Hutt's contributions to economic science were long since highly appreciated by all serious students of social problems. His rank among the outstanding economists of our age is not contested by any competent critic. Yet, what he has written up to now has appealed only to those specializing in the study of economics. This new volume on Keynesianism is addressed not only to specialists, but to all those who want to form a well-grounded opinion concerning the most burning problems of social policies. It is not only a refutation of erroneous doctrines. It is also an exposition of the fundamental principles and ideas of up-to-date economic theory. It is not merely a treatise for the specialist. It is also a book for all those eager to learn what sound economic doctrine has to say about the great problems of our age.